Musings from the Deacon Cave

Deacon Michael Eash, MTS

Copyright © 2021 Deacon Michael Eash

Cover design: Deacon Michael Eash

Author photograph: Wanita Kadolf

Dedication

This book is dedicated to all parish members of St. Bernard in Appleton, Wisconsin past and present who have supported, encouraged, and uplifted me in countless ways as I journey in my vocation as a deacon.

Acknowledgements

First up is my wife Lisa who has been the most wonderful companion a man could ever hope to have as a partner. She is the very definition of "my better half!" Next is my friend Anna who paved the way for me by publishing her first book and has helped me through the process. Foremost is for a loving creator and his son Jesus Christ who has called me to my vocation as a husband and a deacon.

Introduction

It started innocently enough with a memo to the staff from Fr. Dennis asking each staff member to pick a week and write an article for the bulletin. As the "I don't know what to write" and the "I don't have time" started to roll in, it came down to Fr. Dennis and me writing the article every other week. Fr. Amal became our pastor when Fr. Dennis retired and asked if I would write the article while he settled in. Fr. Jude became our pastor when Fr. Amal had to step aside due to a health issue and he asked for me to continue writing the articles and the rest, as they say, is history.

The articles started out with the title *A Letter to the Parishioners*. To distinguish between my articles and those of the pastor's, I changed my title to *Musings from the Deacon Cave*. I have been asked about the title several times and the answer is "yes" there is a deacon cave! It is what Lisa and I call the spare bedroom converted into an office that I work in when Lisa needs to use the living space in our home. Despite the title, it is a very cozy room where I have spent many hours as I went through formation to become a deacon, studying for my undergrad, and then my master's degree. The "deacon cave" came about because it sounds cool, you know, like the "bat cave".

As time went on, I began to receive some positive feedback from parishioners regarding the articles and how much they look forward to reading them each week. Some have told me they cut out the articles to send to friends and family and one parishioner even told me she saves them all! This is what has given me the inspiration to publish the articles that have been written to this date.

About this Book

Since these articles are based on the liturgical calendar and the associated scripture readings, I debated whether to put them in order liturgically, but in the end decided that a chronological order made more sense. Since the main audience for this book is the parishioners of St. Bernard's, leaving them in chronological order allows them to walk through various events that happened in our parish and in our community.

For those unfamiliar with the Roman Catholic calendar for the Sunday readings, it runs on a three-year cycle A, B, and C. (The trick to know the year is that year C evenly divided by three. 2019, for instance, is 2+0+1+9 = 12 / 3 = 4). 2020 then is year A and so forth. Each Sunday is comprised of three readings and a responsorial psalm. Generally, the first reading is from the Old Testament, the second reading is from one the letters in the New Testament, and the third reading is always from one of gospels.

If the article is based on one of the readings, it is indicated at the top of the page. I encourage anyone reading this book to have a bible handy to read the referenced scripture. Not only will it give the article more meaning, but a little scripture reading goes a long way!

Happy reading!
Deacon Mike

Year B
Second Sunday of Advent
December 10, 2017

Isaiah 40:1-5, 9-11

Give Comfort

The reading from Isaiah this week is extolling the great blessings of God upon the Hebrews. *Go up on to a high mountain! Cry at the top of your voice!* Isaiah is telling the people to loudly proclaim what God has done for them. I think that he is, "trying to give credit where credit is due".

Many of us are entering a time when our lives will get very busy. Office parties, shopping, family gatherings, decorating… the "to do" list seems to stretch, while time seems to shrink. While it is good that we are *preparing a way for the Lord* in our lives, we need to remember to give thanks to God as the giver of all good gifts and we need to share that good news with others.

As we check off our "to do" list, we also need to heed the words at the beginning of the reading from Isaiah as well. *Give comfort to my people, says your God.* We need to mindful of those we encounter in our daily lives. Is there someone we know who may be lonely? Is there someone who has recently lost a loved one? Are there family members that need some extra companionship or reassurance?

If we are mindful of those around us and are ready to accompany them, then indeed we can give comfort to God's people.

Advent Blessings,
Deacon Mike

Year B
Christmas
December 25, 2017

God with Us

Is there anything more joyful than to watch a young child anticipating Christmas? Most children know that there is something special about the coming of the baby Jesus and they rarely contain their excitement! As they grow, the wonder of Christmas seems to fade, and as adults, our attention is usually turned towards everything that needs to "get done" and it seems difficult to capture a sense of awe at the coming of our Savior.

What helps me to try and keep the flame of wonder alive is the phrase "Emmanuel"... God With Us. The Creator of the cosmos who is beyond all time cares enough for me and you that he became one of us. He comes to us in all the joys and sorrows of life. He comes to us when we are at our best and when we are at our worst. God is with us always and He sent his Son so that we may know that no matter what... God is with us.

For myself and the entire staff, we pray that this Christmas will find you full of joy, peace, and wonder!

Merry Christmas!
Deacon Mike

Year B
The Epiphany of the Lord
January 7, 2018

What Now?

The celebration of the Epiphany and the Baptism of the Lord
brings the Christmas Season to a close. The anticipation of the
coming of Jesus through Advent and the celebration of his birth
are past. The Church enters into the first section of Ordinary
Time and we seem to just "hang out" until Ash Wednesday. But it
doesn't need to be that way!

Now is a great time to explore your faith! Instead of simply
"hunkering down" for winter, why not join a small group, help out
at church, or volunteer in the community? Take this quiet time of
the year to explore your faith in new ways!

Alpha give everyone the opportunity to do just that! Our "men's
only" group will be starting next Saturday, but there will be more
session starting soon. I'm sure there are many who are thinking,
"enough already with the Alpha!" but I will challenge you to
experience a session yourself before passing judgment.

What now? Get up, bundle up, and come to see what God has in
store for you!

Peace & Blessings,
Deacon Mike

Year B
Third Sunday in Ordinary Time
January 21, 2018

Jonah 3:1-5, 10

Not Me!

In our first reading today, we hear about how Jonah is sent to Nineveh to announce the Lord's message that the town will be destroyed due to its wickedness. This is towards the end of the story of Jonah. The first part of the story tells of how Jonah tried to run away from his mission and ended up in the belly of a fish!

I think that most of us are not very comfortable with the idea of being sent out on a mission from God. For any number of reasons, our first reaction is often, *not me!* We resist the call to spread the Good News to others out of fear, confusion, or just plain indifference. We think "what difference can *I* make"? Jonah said exactly the same thing, and yet by eventually saying "yes" to God, he helped to save the city of Nineveh.

Are we called to go through the streets of Appleton warning of God's coming wrath? Not likely. But we are most certainly called to share the love of God with those around us. Our "Nineveh" may be our workplace, where we shop, and our especially our homes. We are only asked to do what we can do.

If we open ourselves to what God may be asking of us, we can turn our "not me"! to "here I am Lord"!

Deacon Mike

Year B
Fifth Sunday in Ordinary Time
February 4, 2018

Job 7:1-4, 6-7

Why Me?

I think that most adults can relate to Job's lament about his status in life. Even though we may not have gone through everything that Job was subjected to (family killed, livelihood taken, and having a painful skin disease) almost all of us have experienced a time in our life when we questioned, "Is this all that there is?" because we don't think the pain and suffering will ever end. As Job says, "Will I ever see happiness again?!"

As much as we would like to see into the future to see if some relief is coming, we only have hope that indeed things will get better. But there is something else that can offer relief when we are going through a period of trial in our life. In the gospel, Jesus is praying alone when his disciples come to tell him that everyone is looking for him. His response? Let me go preach because <u>this is my purpose</u>.

Even in our times of despair, if we can focus on what God may be needing us to do, it can help to take our mind off our troubles for a least a little while, as we search for *our* purpose. God loves each one of us and has a plan that only *we* can fulfill. Search out that plan. Lent is coming soon, what a great season to devote some time to contemplate what God's plan may be for your life. Sharing your talents and time with others is a great way to turn a time of trial into a time of joy!

Deacon Mike

Year B
First Sunday of Lent
February 18, 2018

Lent Should not be a Four-Letter Word

Every year I am amazed at the amount of people who participate in Ash Wednesday services. When I look out at the congregation, I can't help but think, "Where are all these people on Sunday?!" What is it about the beginning of Lent that makes people come that may not be here on a weekly basis? I believe one of the reasons is because people feel *engaged* with the season of Lent.

Out of all the times of the year, Lent invites *everyone* to *participate* in a special way by preparing our hearts and our minds for the Resurrection of Jesus at Easter. Lent is a season of action and I think that there are many who like the feeling of achievement as they try and live out their own Lenten practices. Sharpening our spiritual discipline through self-denial is a great thing, but if that is all we find meaningful in Lent, are our hearts and minds really changed?

If you haven't in the past, I encourage you to add charitable acts to your Lenten routine. Serving others was one of the central missions of Jesus. He encourages all of us to imitate him by reaching out to others and sharing the love we have been given by him. If we focus on others during Lent, I can almost assure you that Lent will not be a drudgery, but a joy!

Deacon Mike

Year B
Third Sunday of Lent
March 4, 2018

Exodus 20:1-17

The Sabbath

I believe that most of us think of the Sabbath as something that was meant for the Hebrew people a long time ago and it has little relevance today. Let's be real, for those who have jobs, Sunday is the day that is spent getting ready for the next week! I will admit that I am just guilty as anyone for spending Sunday just as busy as any other day. But by doing so am I missing out something more than just "Sunday"? I think the answer is "yes".

Man wasn't created for the Sabbath; the Sabbath was created for man. The notion of keeping one day of the week holy and free from extraneous work is a gift from God to His creatures. He knows that the drive inside most humans to achieve is strong and that we need a day to rest our minds, our hearts, and our bodies. I also know this is easier said than done.

I would encourage those who are not able to use Sunday as a day of rest to at least find some way of making the day special. Sit, at least for a little while, turn off the television, enjoy a book or magazine, enjoy nature… whatever it takes to slow down and spend a little time with God. After all,… he made the day for _you_!

Deacon Mike

Year B
Fifth Sunday of Lent
March 18, 2018

John 12:20-33

Growing Wheat

Since we live in the Midwest and are around farming, when we hear Jesus talking about the grain of wheat that must fall to the ground and die in order to become fruitful… we get that… just as the original hearers would have! For more wheat to be grown, a select number of grains need to be forced into the earth so that more grain can flourish… the process is amazing.

The question for us is, "What is *our* grain?"

Is it our talent? What would happen if we would all give some more time to helping others? By sharing our talents with others, wouldn't we see some amazing results?

Is it our treasure? During this Lenten season, can we give just a little bit more? By planting some of our money, wouldn't we see some amazing results?

Is it our time in prayer? If we spend some more time in prayer, wouldn't we see some amazing results?

Lent will be over soon. Can we use the remaining time to plant some of our talent, treasure, and time? Can we let these "grains" fall to the ground and die so that more grain can flourish?

Deacon Mike

Year B
Easter Sunday
April 1, 2018

Responsorial Psalm

Let Us Rejoice and Be Glad!

Easter is such a wonderful time of the year. Not only do we get to dispense with the rigors of Lent, but once Easter arrives, we know that warmer weather is not far behind! Soon the earth will be sprouting forth with plants of all shapes, sizes, and colors. The trees will begin to sprout their leaves. The grass will soon be turning green and we can begin to leave our layers of outerwear in the closet!

This is the type of joy that the psalmist is describing. Being joyful for the richness and diversity of life and the opportunity to be witness to all that God has created! Easter is also the perfect time to give thanks to God for the gift of Jesus to humanity. God comes to us as friend, counsellor, savior, brother, and Lord in the person of Jesus. The best part... he is still ALIVE and very much a part of our lives!

For any visitors with us this weekend, the entire staff and community of St. Bernard gives you a warm welcome and invitation to join us whenever you can. For those joining us who are not so sure about the whole "church" thing (or even those who are)... why not try Alpha? Bring your doubts, your fears, and your curiosity and see what Jesus might have in store for *you!*

Easter Blessings!
Deacon Mike

Year B
Divine Mercy Sunday
April 8, 2018

John 20:19-31

Peace be with You

We hear these words spoken by Jesus to his disciples. It is a phrase that we recognize from our participation at Mass. But how often do we hear this phrase outside of Mass? Why is that?

Extending the peace of Christ to others can change conversations, can change interactions, and can relationships. Jesus spoke it often to his followers and even instructed the Apostles to extend that greeting whenever they entered a new town or home. They were told that if the peace was accepted that they were welcomed and should stay there. If the peace was rejected, they were promised it would flow back to them so that they would have their peace doubled!

How many times do we get in heated conversations with those close to us and fail to realize that the peace of Jesus is available to us? Using these words goes beyond just wishing someone well, we are actually calling upon the Spirit of Christ to be present in the situation.

So the next time you find yourself in a situation that is growing tense, why not extend the peace of Christ to the other person and see what happens!

May the Peace of Christ be with You!
Deacon Mike

Year B
Third Sunday of Easter
April 15, 2018

Luke 24:35-48

You Are Witnesses of These Things

At the end of the gospel today, Jesus does two things. He opens the minds of the apostles to understand the scriptures about the Messiah, and then he helps them understand that *they* are the ones who are witnesses that *he* is the Messiah. He is telling them that their witnessing will be very important! Although this witnessing begins with apostles, it certainly doesn't end there.

As Christians, we witness Jesus working in our lives and the life of the Church, but much like the apostles in the gospel, do we fail to recognize how we have been chosen to be witnesses? The question is, "Do we see how Jesus is working in our life?"

As followers of Jesus, we should strive to be aware of how his presence in our lives is making a difference, not only for us, but for those around us too. It is wonderful that we have Jesus as our friend and savior, but if keep it to ourselves we may deprive others of coming to know Jesus. The apostles were chosen to be witnesses of the works of Jesus so that they could share the Good News with the world… we are chosen to be witnesses to do the same!

Easter Blessings,
Deacon Mike

Year B
Fifth Sunday of Easter
April 29, 2018

John 15:1-8

Fruit is Good for You!

Both Lisa and I "brown bag" our lunches during the week. Lisa assembles our lunches with loving care, always making sure that we have a well-balanced meal. Vegetables and fruit are always included to supply the necessary vitamins and nutrients we need to make it through the day. On occasion, a serving of fruit will make its way back home and I am usually reminded that it is important to have enough servings of fruit because "It's good for you."

In today's gospel, Jesus uses the analogy that he is the vine and his followers (we) are branches that need to produce good fruit. When we stay attached to Jesus, he supplies us with the nutrients we need to continue to grow and bear good fruit. Jesus also uses some pretty strong imagery of what happens if we do not remain attached to him… we begin to wither and are burned up.

There are many in our world who are withering. They are attached to vines that do not supply what is needed to produce good fruit. That is why it is so important that we stay attached to the Vine so that we can produce the fruit that is needed for everyone. Fruit is good for you, and being good fruit is good for everyone!

Deacon Mike

Year B
The Ascension of the Lord
May 13, 2018

Acts 1:1-11

Not Knowing? Get Going!

In our first reading today, the apostles ask Jesus if now is the time for him to restore the kingdom to Israel. His response, of course, is that it is not for them to know the times or the seasons that the Father has established. But that is not the end of his instruction. He immediately tells them that with the help of the Holy Spirit, they will be going out into the world to proclaim the Good News. There is an important dynamic going on here that I think we can apply to our lives.

Whenever we encounter times of uncertainty in our life, it is easy to want to sit back and await the outcome before we move on. We think that we will have a clearer picture of what lies ahead and that life will be better. However, if we take our cue from the reading, what we should do is call on the Holy Spirit and GO! Not necessarily on what we are waiting on, but simply get out and do some good.

Not knowing is hard and the more serious the matter, the harder it becomes. Doing nothing usually makes the waiting harder because we draw into ourselves and become consumed by our imagination of all the possible outcomes. But if we move away from ourselves and towards others, we are in a better position to handle the outcome, no matter what it happens to be.

So, the next time you find yourself not knowing what will happen… get going! Write an old friend, visit an elderly neighbor, sign up for a small group. See what happens when we GO!

Deacon Mike

Year B
The Most Holy Trinity
May 27, 2018

Romans 8:14-17

We Are Children of God

One day when my niece was around two years old, she was staying at my parent's house for the day. When it came time for grandpa to go to work, she pleaded with him to play "hockey." After having her repeat herself several times, it finally came to light that she wanted him to play "hooky" and stay home from work so he could play with her for the day.

I think that we are kind of like that with God sometimes. We know what we want to say to him, but it just doesn't come out quite right. We struggle for the words as we contemplate in our hearts what we think we need from him. I think that sometimes, we just need to remember that we are children of God, and just like any good parent (or grandparent), God will listen to us repeat ourselves until we finally get it right.

Let us always remember that we are children of God and can approach him with everything that is in our hearts, even if we don't have all the right words!

Finally, may all those who served our country receive a special blessing for their service!

Deacon Mike

Year B
Tenth Sunday in Ordinary Time
June 10, 2018

Mark 3:20-35

Whoever Does the Will of God

Every Saturday evening at 6:30, between 65 – 75 men gather for
Catholic liturgy at the Oshkosh State Correctional Institution (the
one right beside Interstate 41). There are two priests that
volunteer to say Mass one weekend a month and the other
Saturdays are taken by deacons who lead the gathering using
the rites of Sunday Celebration in the Absence of a Priest
(formally known as Liturgy of the Word with Communion.) Bishop
Ricken makes it a point to celebrate with the inmates during
Advent and Lent as well.

One of my ministries is to coordinate the scheduling of the
priests, deacons, and bishop along with leading liturgy as my
turn comes up in the schedule. This ministry has been a great
blessing for me because I can see the enthusiasm of those
bringing Jesus to the inmates and I can see the enthusiasm of
the inmates as they encounter Jesus through Scripture and
Communion in their shared community.

But ministering to those in need is not just a "clergy" thing. There
is little doubt that regardless of the circumstances, we
are *all* called to minister to those less fortunate than ourselves…
indeed that is the will of God! So, I encourage you this summer
to find a ministry that will help make a difference in the lives of
others (and yourself as well!)

Summer Blessings,
Deacon Mike

Year B
Eleventh Sunday in Ordinary Time
June 17, 2018

Ezekiel 17:22-24 / Mark 4:26-34

Home Grown

Anyone who gardens is usually thrilled with this time of year. The work of planting, weeding, fertilizing, and tending all of the beds is rewarded with new growth and blooms! In our first reading from Ezekiel, God even plays the part of gardener by planting trees. In the gospel, the parable of the mustard seed continues the theme of planting and growing. Both readings seem very appropriate for this time of year.

Beyond the literal reading, however, these readings should help us to think about the way that we plant and cultivate in the relationships in our lives. Are we good gardeners with our relationships? Do we do the work of helping our relationships grow or do we leave them to chance? Just like plants need care for them to reach their full potential, relationships require care to make them thrive. This is especially true in our relationships with other family members. In order for a family to bloom, there needs to be the work of weeding, fertilizing, and watering. Good family relationships should not be left to chance!

This summer take some time to literally "stop and smell the roses"! Enjoy the creation that is all around us. But also take some time to enjoy the relationships in your life. Just like a beautiful flower can bring some joy into life, beautiful relationships can bring great joy!

Deacon Mike

Year B
The Nativity of Saint John the Baptist
June 24, 2018

Farwell to Fr. Dennis Ryan

Thank You Fr. Dennis

Though I thought I had toiled in vain, and for nothing, uselessly, spent my strength, yet my reward is with the LORD, my recompense is with my God. Isaiah 49:4.

It seems almost surreal that this is the last week that Fr. Dennis will be our pastor at St. Bernard's. For thirteen years we have been blessed to have a pastor so committed to growing our parish and helping us grow in our faith life. Anyone who has worked with Fr. Dennis on a committee knows that he has a passion for this parish that not everyone gets a chance to see.

In his time here, Fr. Dennis has helped us to celebrate our weddings and baptisms. He has helped our children grow through receiving the Sacraments for the first time. He has helped us say goodbye to our loved ones. He has journeyed with us through our good times and bad always providing a steady shoulder to lean on.

Year B
Fourteenth Sunday in Ordinary Time
July 8, 2018

Welcome of Fr. Amal Roche

Welcome Fr. Amal!

One of the most constant things in life is that there is change!
For some, change is exciting. Full of new possibilities and the
expectation of what could happen. For others, change is hard.
Most of us like to know with some certainty what will happen
next, especially in our faith life. Some are ambivalent to change
thinking that what ever happens, happens and they will adapt to
whatever comes next. There is no right or wrong in any of these
views, but it is good to keep in mind that not everyone adapts to
change in the same way.

A new chapter begins this week in the life of our parish. We
welcome Fr. Amal Roche as our new leader to help us write our
stories as we fill in the pages of this new chapter. Some of the
stories will be full of joy, others of sadness, and through it all, Fr.
Amal will learn our stories and we will learn his. We will help
each other write our stories as people of God, searching for the
paths that we are called to tread.

Welcome to our family Fr. Amal! Just like any family we have our
good moments and not so good moments, but through it all we
are still family. We are joyful that the Lord has chosen you to join
our family and we look forward to what the future has in store for
all of us!

Year B
Seventeenth Sunday in Ordinary Time
July 29, 2018

John 6:1-15

Musings from the Deacon Cave

Fr. Amal asked if I could take over this column for a while, so he can focus on getting settled into his work flow at the parish. He will still be writing occasionally, but it looks like you are stuck with me for the most part.

You may be curious about the title change. The bedroom that Lisa and I converted into a den/study is affectionately known at the "Deacon Cave." (It makes it sound cool like the Bat Cave.) It is the place where I can go to do homework or work on homilies so that I am not occupying more prime areas of the house with my "accessories." (In other words, I am not taking up space in the living room!) The room has a mixture of sports and religious memorabilia and is a great place for me to collect my thoughts.

Everyone needs to have their own special place for being able to sit, pray, and think. In our gospel reading today, Jesus feeding the five thousand gets all the attention, and what may be missed is that he was trying to get away from the crowds when he went up on the mountain. Jesus knew the importance of having some time alone… to get away from the crowds. What about us? Do we take the time to step away from the busyness of life to think and to pray? If it was good for Jesus, it should be good for us as well!

Deacon Mike

Year B
Eighteenth Sunday in Ordinary Time
August 5, 2018

Exodus 16:2-4, 12-15

God Hears Our Grumblings

In the reading from Exodus today, the Israelites were complaining to Moses and Aaron that they did not have enough to eat. (This comes after their complaint that they didn't have enough water to drink.) God hears their complaints and gives them an abundance of quail for flesh and manna for bread. God is showing his people that he is with them and he wants them to trust that he has a plan for their community.

I know that I can become much like the Israelites in the story today. Even though I have witnessed God working in my life I still complain that I don't have it as good as I think I should. The fact, however, is that I have always had my basics needs met and usually much beyond! I often have to ask myself, "What do I really have to complain about?" The answer comes back… "nothing!" And yet in a few minutes my list of complaints is already growing! Through it all, I know that God hears my grumblings.

God hears all of our grumblings, but he also hears all of our laughter! When we can start to put aside our list of complaints, we have more room for the joy that only Jesus can provide. When we open our hearts to let Jesus in, our grumblings turn into laughter! It is not to say that we will not encounter struggles in our life, but with Jesus at our side, what do we really have to complain about?

Deacon Mike

Year B
Nineteenth Sunday in Ordinary Time
August 12, 2018

1 Kings 19:4-8

Strength for the Journey

In the first reading today, Elijah was ready to throw in towel and call it quits. The struggles that he had encountered were just too much for him and he could not bear to go on. But God had more work for Elijah to do and so he sent an angel to feed Elijah so that he would have the strength to continue his journey.

There are many people in the world today that feel like Elijah. They feel like their struggles are just too much to bear and they would rather see their life end than to carry on. The feeling of despair can claim anyone. It can affect people from all walks of life and can even affect those who appear to "have it all together."

In the reading from Kings, God sent an angel to help Elijah past his despair. As Christians, we are called to be that angel for others. We are *all* called to be healers in the world through our words and our actions. We accomplish this foremost by building up those around us rather than tearing them down. We should treat those around us with respect and compassion even though we feel they may be unworthy of either.

We also accomplish our mission as healers by being there for others. A kind word, a smile, words of encouragement can impact others in profound ways. Small acts of kindness not only strengthen others for their journey but can help us on our journey as well.

Deacon Mike

Year B
Twentieth Sunday in Ordinary Time
August 19, 2018

Ephesians 5:15-20

Making the Most of Opportunity

In Paul's letter the Ephesians today, he encourages them to live wisely and to get rid of the things that will hinder their growth with God.

There are not many of us who do not have indulgences that hinder our willingness to grow closer to God. It may be an addiction to alcohol, gambling, or drugs. It may be more subtle like spending too much time engaged with sports or shopping. It may be that we spend too much time with our electronic devices and not enough time with our families. There are not many of us who escape from distractions that lead us away from deepening our relationship with God and with others.

That is why Paul uses some strong language to remind the Ephesians that they need to make the most of the opportunity to grow in their faith. Paul knows that our time on earth is limited, and if we do not take advantage of the opportunities to grow closer to God, we are missing out on what we are created for.

Let us heed Paul's words and live wisely… not foolishly. Make the most of every opportunity to grow in your faith!

Deacon Mike

Year B
Twenty-first Sunday in Ordinary Time
August 26, 2018

Joshua 24:1-2a, 15-17, 18 / John 6:60-69

Choices, Choices, Choices

There isn't a day that goes by that we do not make choices. Even deciding not to make a choice is a choice! Most choices are fairly easy to make and have very little impact one way or another. But there are some choices that we make that have much larger implications.

In the first reading today, Joshua forces Israel to make a choice by telling them to decide whether they are going to serve the Lord or the gods of Egypt. Joshua knows that in order for Israel to move forward as a people they have to decide what they are going to be about.

In the Gospel today, after many of Jesus' disciples abandoned him, he puts the apostles to the test by asking them if their choice is to leave also. We hear Peter's response that they are committed to Jesus.

I think we often drift through our faith life trying to avoid choices. The most basic of which is whether we are committed to following Jesus or not. Events in life can throw us many challenges and it is not always easy to act the way we should. We can choose to let things in our life weigh us down or we can choose to let Jesus into all aspects of our life. What is our choice?

Deacon Mike

Year B
Twenty-second Sunday in Ordinary
September 9, 2018

James 1:17-18, 21b-22, 27

James the Teacher

In the second reading today, James tells the community how we tend to treat others that we think are "below us." We seek the attention of those we think are cool and ignore those we think are not cool. I think that this is particularly important to those who are in school.

For many, going to school is the first experience of encountering others that may be different than themselves. We interact with those who may look different, sound different, or act different than we experience at home. How do we treat those that are different than us?

When we encounter those that are different than us, do we reach out to them or do we ignore them? Do we talk about them poorly or do we defend them when others may be saying things that are not so nice? Do we have the courage to reach out to those that may be in most need of a friend?

James would be the first to say that this is not easy, but that is exactly what Jesus calls us to do. So, whether we are in school (or many years beyond school) let us pray that we have a generous spirit and reach out to those that may need us to be a friend.

Deacon Mike

Year B
Twenty-third Sunday in Ordinary Time
September 16, 2018

James 2:1-5

Where the Rubber Meets the Road

Chances are that we have all heard the phrase "where the rubber meets the road" (or something close to it.) It references that no matter what kind of engine or transmission that a car may have, it all comes down to the tires putting all that energy into contact with the road to move the car forward. A car can have all kinds of power, but if the tires don't contact the road, the car will just sit there with the tires spinning.

In the second reading today, St. James talks about faith and works. He says that having faith is great and needed, but if faith is not put into practice it is kind of worthless. It is like having a fast car with bald tires… it looks nice, but it really doesn't do much! So what are we to take away from this reading?

The first thing is that having faith in Jesus Christ is crucial. James does not dismiss anyone who has strong faith because he knows that faith in Jesus is the bedrock of our spiritual lives. But how we live out our faith shows how much (or little) faith we really have. If we fail to take care of those around us, then we are missing the point of what our faith life is all about.

Our faith is only truly alive when we share it with others. Prayer and piety can be the engine and transmission of our spiritual lives but putting that faith into practice is where the rubber truly meets the road!

Deacon Mike

Year B
Twenty-fourth Sunday in Ordinary Time
September 23, 2018

James 2:14-18

Jealousy or Peace?

The last few weeks the second reading has been from the book of James. If there is ever a no-nonsense, tell-it-like-it-is guy… it is James. He doesn't spend much time mincing words or elaborating some drawn-out theology… he calls it like he sees it. I like the book of James, because it calls me to do what is right.

This week's reading from James is no different. He doesn't pull any punches by saying that where jealousy and selfish ambition exist, there is disorder. It is easy to gloss over this sentence with a simple acknowledgment that it is true, but does it hold true for you in your life? Have there been times when being jealous or envious of someone else has ended poorly? Usually the answer is "yes."

James doesn't just stop there… he offers a remedy; to seek God's wisdom which displaces disorder and replaces it with peace, mercy, and good fruits. When we are being true to ourselves and who we are, then there is a genuine peace in our lives and we receive much from God because we learn to ask rightly.

So, this week, take some time to ask God to help you examine your life to see if there are areas where jealousy and envy have made a home. If we ask for God's wisdom, then we are open to receive what will put our lives in order and we can reap the rewards of cultivating a peace that will help us and those around us.

Deacon Mike

Year B
Twenty-fifth Sunday in Ordinary Time
September 30, 2018

Mark 9:30-37

Even the Smallest Deeds Matter

Buried in the gospel today, Jesus tells his disciples that, "Anyone who gives you a cup of water to drink because you belong to Christ, amen, I say to you, will surely not lose his reward."

I think that there are times when we think that we have to do something big or grand in order to make a difference. If our time and resources are such… that is great! But we must also keep in mind that the little things also matter.

I read a story recently that a young woman had to evacuate her apartment in South Carolina due to Hurricane Florence. She was leaving a restaurant in Florida and noticed a note on her car windshield. She expected it to be nasty note about her parking. Instead the hand-written letter said, "Saw your license plate is from South Carolina. Not sure if you evacuated from the storm, but just know Florida is praying for you and your state." There was also a small gift card attached.

This small act of kindness had a tremendous impact on the young woman who eventually tracked down the person who left the note to thank her in person. She is also looking for ways to pay it forward to someone else.

Help with the big things when you can, but always remember that even the smallest deeds matter! (Even a cup of water!)

Deacon Mike

Year B
Twenty-sixth Sunday in Ordinary Time
October 7, 2018

Mark 9:38-43, 45, 47-48

Love Like a Child

At the end of the gospel today, Jesus is giving us instructions on how to enter God's kingdom in reverse. He tells his followers that whoever does not accept the kingdom of God like a child will not enter into it. So, what is it about a child's willingness to accept God's kingdom that we might be able to apply to our own faith?

First, children are curious. If you have ever spent any time around a two or three-year-old, you have probably been inundated with the question "why?" many times! Children are relentless in having their curiosity satisfied. As adults we tend to rank our questions in order of importance. We work on the ones we think are important and leave the rest. The problem is that we think we know what is important. Maybe we do… but then again maybe we don't! If we make a habit of asking "why?" about our faith (and getting the answer) we will grow tremendously in our faith!

Next, children have a level of trust that adults rarely possess. For many adults, life is challenging. Over time, we build up barriers of protection so that we don't get hurt. But those barriers can also keep out those that want what is best for us… even God. We need to find ways of helping us come to know that God wants what is best for us. Just like a loving parent wants what is best for their children. We need to be able to trust our Creator.

Finally, children love to love. Children find great joy in new relationships and new adventures and are eager to learn to love others. Lisa and I have two little neighbor girls and every time they see us outside they are so excited to tell us what they are doing. They are ready to share their joy with us even though we only interact across the fence! Sharing our love and our joy with others is a lesson we can learn from children!

So be curious in your faith, trust that God wants what is best for you, and share your love with others. Then you will be ready to accept the kingdom of God like a child!

Deacon Mike

Year B
Twenty-seventh Sunday in Ordinary Time
October 14, 2018

Genesis 2:18-24 / Psalm 140

A Word to the Wise

If you were able to be granted a wish, what would it be? I am
sure that most of us have pondered the possibility at one time or
another (at least in passing.) We could ask for all kinds of things,
both selfish (I want to be rich) and unselfish (good health for my
family.) We could ask for something huge like world peace!

What about wisdom?

This probably wouldn't be at the top of my list, but we find a
couple of examples of exactly that in our liturgy today! In the first
verse of the responsorial psalm, the psalmist asks for God to
teach us to number our days correctly so that we may gain
wisdom of heart. In the first reading today, the author prayed and
pleaded for prudence and wisdom even above all the gold and
silver in the world! Why is wisdom so valued in our readings?

Wisdom brings together our experience, knowledge, and good
judgment for the betterment, not just of ourselves, but of
everyone. Wisdom reaches beyond our personal wishes so that
we can live justly and rightly as we walk with Jesus and each
other. Wisdom brings peace to our lives and to those around us,
and even into the world.

In a world that seems to thrive on conflict and unrest, asking God
for wisdom may be just the thing we need to "shine like the stars
in the sky!"

Deacon Mike

Year B
Twenty-eighth Sunday in Ordinary Time
October 21, 2018

Hebrews 4:12-13

Jesus Knows

There are not too many of us that can go through life without
experiencing some sort of pain. For some it is physical pain, for
others emotional pain, and for others it is the pain of knowing
they are different, and they don't feel like they fit in. In the end, it
doesn't matter… pain is pain, and it can affect us in how we view
ourselves and how we interact with others.

In the reading to the Hebrews today, the author says that, "we do
not have a high priest who is unable to sympathize with our
weaknesses, but one who has similarly been tested in every
way…" In other words, Jesus is there for us because he knows
our pain.

He knows what it like to be abandoned by those he trusted most.
He knows what it is like to experience intense physical pain as
his hands and feet were pierced with nails. He knows what it is
like to be ridiculed for being different than those around him.

Jesus knows.

But Jesus also knows that the pain of this world does not need to
be in vain. It is very common that those that experience pain are
the ones who can most easily comfort others in their pain
because they have been there themselves. Just as Jesus can
sympathize with us, we can sympathize with others. The
question is: can we accept our pain and reach out to others or do
we let our pain define who we are and retreat into ourselves?

Jesus knows.

Deacon Mike

Year B
Twenty-ninth Sunday in Ordinary Time
October 28, 2018

All Saints Day / All Souls Day

All Hallows Eve

It is that time of year again when all the ghosts, goblins, princesses, firefighters, and the like move from house to house asking for some goodies for their bags. It also may seem like the last hurrah before we retreat into our houses for the coming winter. But for Christians, it should also be a time of thanksgiving.

First, we celebrate All-Saint's Day on Thursday. A chance for us to celebrate and honor those men and women who came before us that are now in the Kingdom. Friday is All-Souls day when we remember all those that have gone before us. It should bring us great joy to remember all those that have blessed our lives and helped to make us who we are today.

So, as we celebrate Halloween, let us take time to remember that the Lord has done great things for us in the relationships we have experienced. Let us always remember those that have gone before us!

By the way… do you know how to scare a cow?   "BOO cow!"

This is just a joke.

Deacon Mike

Year B
Thirty-first Sunday in Ordinary Time
November 4, 2018

Mark 12:28b-34

It's Found in the Journey

In the gospel today, Jesus has a conversation with a scribe
about what is the most important commandment. Jesus'
response is a familiar one; Love your God and love your
neighbor. The scribe responds affirmatively that indeed these are
the greatest of the commandments. Jesus says that the man is
not far from the kingdom of God. This is one of the few times that
Jesus comes right out and says what is needed to enter the
kingdom of God… this may deserve some attention!

Most of us can understand why these are the most important
commandments, but what do we do with them? Do we just read
them and move on, or do we let the words soak in and actually
move our hearts to accept these commandments as more than
just words on a page? Where do we even begin to incorporate
these commandments into our lives?

Maybe a good place to start is to think of these commandments
as part of our journey and not just the end destination. Can we
think of ways of incorporating our love for God in our daily lives?
What about a simple prayer of thanksgiving to God when we
wake up in the morning and a prayer of thanksgiving to God
when we go to bed at night? Like all journeys… it has to start
somewhere!

Deacon Mike

Year B
Thirty-third Sunday in Ordinary Time
November 18, 2018

Daniel 12:1-3

The Wise Shine Brightly

We have been reading a lot about wisdom lately. Although today's first reading isn't from the book of Wisdom, it still touches on the subject. At the end of the reading from Daniel today, there is a proclamation that the wise will shine brightly and that those who lead others to justice will shine like the stars. So maybe the question that we should ask is, "are we wise?"

Do we value the things in life that are important, or do we spend our time and energy on things that are fleeting? Are we about Prayer or Packers? Are we about Discipleship Nights or Dancing with the Stars? Are we about Relationships or Racing? Now of course, there is a place in our lives for all these things. It is not about either/or, but about what we value as important. A good measure if we are making wise choices is to follow the advice that wisdom always looks towards what will last.

Spending time in prayer with God, working on deepening our faith, and building good, healthy, relationships are wise choices because all of them will last… but it doesn't happen by accident. We need to be conscious that our daily choices matter. We also need to work on being aware of what God might be calling us to do that we haven't in the past.

Let us all work on building up wisdom in our lives so that we can shine like the stars!

Deacon Mike

Year C
Second Sunday of Advent
December 9, 2018

Philippians 1:4-6, 8-11

Discern What is Valuable

We are entering the heart of the Advent season which means that we are also in the heart of the Christmas rush season. If you are like me, the two seem to be in constant competition for my time and energy. Advent season calls me into prayer, reflection, and a quieter spirit. The Christmas rush season tends to call me to hurried-ness, anxiety, and a restless spirit. Both call me to be prepared but for entirely different things.

In the second reading today, Paul tells the Philippians that he prays that their love may increase ever more in knowledge and every kind of perception, and to discern what is of value.

There is no doubt that Christmas is a time of great joy for Christians. It is right that we should celebrate that our Creator chose to become one of us! It is also good that we find joy in celebrating this feast with our friends and family! But I think we should heed Paul's advice and discern what is of value. Do we find value in preparing our heart and mind for the coming of our Savior or do we find value in the "stuff" of Christmas?

There is no need to feel anxious if we feel our focus is not where it should be. There is still plenty of time in this Advent season to re-balance our lives if we feel that we have lost touch with what is truly valuable. Let us remember that Jesus IS the reason for the season!

Deacon Mike

Year C
Third Sunday of Advent
December 16, 2018

Philippians 4:4-7

Being Anxious

While the Christmas season can bring great joy for many, it can also bring much anxiety for some. Not just a peripheral anxiousness about not being able to get everything done, but a deep-seated anxiety. I have seen recent postings on Facebook for concrete steps to help people deal with an anxiety attack that suggest finding tangible things to focus on. Finding things that the person can see, touch, and smell as a way of grounding and giving the person a sense of control.

I also sense there are many who have a spiritual anxiety. Having access to real-time events around the world can be informative, but it can also be overwhelming. The media is quick to bring tragedy after tragedy (literally) right into our hands and offer opinion after opinion about who is to blame. It can be easy to slip into chronic anxiousness.

In the letter to the Philippians today, Paul says that we to have no anxiety all. Paul's remedy is similar to that of addressing an anxiety attack… focus on what is close by. Paul says it clearly… our hope is in Jesus.

Soon we will celebrate the coming of a little baby to a manger in Bethlehem, but we are also celebrating the coming of our King! A King destined to rule the world! So indeed, let us make our requests know to God, but also never forget that our hearts should be at rest because our Lord IS near!

Advent Blessings!
Deacon Mike

Year C
The Holy Family of Jesus, Mary and Joseph
December 30. 2018

Family Ties

There was a sitcom that aired in the 1980s that was named
Family Ties. It was situated around a family that was rather
diverse in ideology with the parents cast as hippies left over from
the sixties and the oldest son (Alex P. Keaton) aspiring to
everything conservative. The show would play upon the
differences within the family, but at the end of the episodes the
family always became the most important thing.

Today we celebrate the feast of the Holy Family. After coming off
of the excitement of Christmas, this celebration can get lost in
the shuffle, but we do ourselves a disfavor if we do not take
some time to reflect on this feast day. For me one of the things
that this day reminds me of is how our God chose to be a part of
a human family. Our God reaffirms that where we find love,
where we find ourselves, and where we find God is within the
messy-ness of family.

We need to mindful though that there are those who are alone or
are not in contact with their family. That is where our parish
family comes in. We need to remember that no matter the
differences in our situations or in our ideologies, in the end, what
matters is that we are a family. Let us take the opportunity to
build each other up and help each other in our quest to someday
join the Holy Family in heaven!

May all of our families be blessed in a special way in the new
year!

Deacon Mike

Year C
The Epiphany of the Lord
January 6, 2019

Matthew 2:1-12

Seeing is More Than Just Believing

Today we celebrate the Epiphany of the Lord. Most of us have heard the story of the magi so many times, it can become just a nice story of how three prominent men traveled a long distance to see a new king. We add to the story ourselves by allowing our imagination to think about what it might have been like to witness this encounter. We can begin to think this is what the Epiphany is about.

But the Epiphany is deeper than just a story about some men coming to see Jesus. We do not know much about the magi, but we do know that their encounter with Jesus changed them. It changed them so much that they avoided returning to Herod which would have put them at great risk. Their encounter was more than just a seeing of Jesus. It should be the same with us.

Through our own epiphany of Jesus, we may deepen our prayer life or find ways of encountering Jesus in others. One thing we can do for sure is to pray to the Lord and ask him to come to us in new ways this coming year. Epiphany is more than just believing… it is about being open to an encounter with Jesus that changes our hearts and minds.

May God bless all of us in a special way in 2019!

Deacon Mike

Year C
The Baptism of the Lord
January 13, 2019

Acts 10:34-38

God was with Him

In our second reading today, the author gives a synopsis of how
God sent Jesus into the world to do good, preach peace, and to
heal. At the end of our reading, the author says, "For God was
with him." The gospel reading reaffirms this when after Jesus is
baptized, a voice from heaven says that "You are beloved Son
with you I am well pleased." I think that it is easy for us to read
these passages as a way of reaffirming our belief that Jesus is
the Son of God, but there is something here that can be applied
to all of us.

We need to remember that God is with <u>us</u> too! God is with us
always, but I think that he is with us in a special way when we go
about doing good, preaching peace, and healing. While it is true
that not all of us have the gift of giving physical healing, we all
have the ability to give emotional and spiritual healing to others
through our words and actions. We can all certainly go about
doing good and preaching peace!

One of the essential elements of being Christian is to try our best
to follow in the footsteps of Jesus. There are many who find this
an impossible example of how to live and they do not even try.
There are others who do not even consider following Jesus
because of the actions of those who claim they are Christians
but do not follow his teachings. We need to remember that we
are not called to be perfect, but only to share ourselves with
others… even in our incompleteness.

If we do good, preach peace, and bring healing to others as best
we can, God indeed will be with us!

Deacon Mike

Year C
Second Sunday in Ordinary Time
January 20, 2019

1 Corinthians 12:4-11

Both/And   not   Either/Or

It seems like we are given a steady dose of conflict through the media these days. The formula is not hard to figure out… conflict increases interest which increases exposure for advertisers. Our current system for delivering information is kind of built on conflict. This isn't a problem in itself, but over time it can influence our thinking that there are only either/or choices and either/or outcomes. This is a problem because we eventually lose the ability to see the world as needing a wider vision to take in its complexity.

That is what Paul is trying to combat in the second reading today to the Corinthians. He starts out by reminding the listener that there are different gifts, service, and workings, but they all come from the same source. Next, he lists nine different gifts of the spirit that can be given to people of faith. Each and every spiritual gift is given for some benefit. There is no singular gift that is above the others… they are each important. He is telling them (and us) that we do not live in an "either/or" world, but a "both/and" world! So how do we see ourselves?

Do we judge others because they are different from us or do we see others as having gifts that we may not have ourselves? Do we spend our time focused on conflict or do we look for what unites us? What do we do to cultivate our own unique gifts as a response to God's gifts to us? If we use our energy to affirm the gifts of others and share our gifts freely, we can move beyond either/or and celebrate both/and!

Deacon Mike

Year C
Third Sunday in Ordinary Time
January 27, 2019

Nehemiah 8:2-4a, 5-6, 8-10

Living Large

In the reading today from Nehemiah, the story is told of Ezra explaining the Torah (the Law) to the assembly of Israelites. The reading tells of the fashion in which Ezra unrolled the scroll so that all could see and explained the scriptures so that everyone could understand. The imagery in this reading provides us with enough detail to know that the reading of the Law was a grand event that was celebrated by the people.

What this story has recalled for me is to question, "how often do I read scripture in a grand fashion?" Okay, not building a special platform and calling all my neighbors to listen to me read from the bible (although that might be interesting) but really sitting down and reading from scripture with my mind and heart ready to understand? Setting up a special environment like a favorite chair, something to drink, and the right lighting to really focus on the word of God?

We can probably all agree that we live in a fast-paced world of constant change. I think what gets missed sometimes is the ability to really appreciate life, and especially our faith life. So let's take some time this week to pump up our faith life! Maybe through prayer, scripture, or some good deeds. Ezra has it right… sometimes we need to live large!

Deacon Mike

Year C
Fourth Sunday in Ordinary Time
February 3, 2019

1 Corinthians 12:31—13:13

The Gong Show

I see that they have resurrected *The Gong Show*. For those of us who are "more mature" we can recall the original *Gong Show* from the 70's. The premise of both shows is the same. An armature act gets on stage, and a panel of three judges can get up at any time during the performance and clang a giant gong which tells the act that they are not up to snuff, and their time is done.

In Paul's letter to the Corinthians today, we hear the passage where he talks about love. Not infatuation or sensual love, but real Christian love for others. After his description of what love is and is not, he urges the Corinthians to give up their old ways by describing how a child believes in childish things, but adults should give up childish things… they should grow in their faith life.

I know for me that there are times when I still do (spiritually) childish things. I become angry, jealous, and most of the list of what Paul says is not love. I am probably not alone in this. When we start to think that way, we need to have our own "gong" that we can ring to tell us that we are not up to snuff, and our time is done! If we can recognize those times when we are not thinking and acting like we should and work to change it, then we can put aside childish things and begin to see clearly that what is above all is love. Love of God, love of self, and love of others.

The Unknown Deacon

Year C
Fifth Sunday in Ordinary Time
February 10, 2019

Isaiah 6:1-2a, 3-8 and 1 Corinthians 15:1-11

Worthy to Serve?

I think that there are a few (many?) (most?) people who do not feel worthy to serve in the Church. Many times, I have heard phrases like, "I do not know enough to help," "I am too shy," "I have done too many bad things in my life," or "I am not holy enough." Do any of these sound familiar? If you have found yourself saying any of these things to yourself, you are in good company!

In the first reading today, Isaiah cries out that he is, "a man with unclean lips." In the second reading, Paul says he is, "the least of the apostles" and that he is, "not worthy to be called an apostle." Let that sink in for just a moment. Isaiah and Paul both felt unworthy to serve God! After acknowledging their shortcomings and sinfulness, how did they respond?

Isaiah says, "Here I am; 'send me!'" Paul says that, "through the grace of God… I have toiled harder than the others."

Instead of focusing on what keeps them from serving, they say "yes!" for the sake of serving God and serving others. There is a saying that, "God does not call the qualified, he qualifies those who are called." If we give God our "yes!" he will be with us to give us what we need to serve. We are all worthy to serve!

Deacon Mike

Year C
Sixth Sunday in Ordinary Time
February 17, 2019

Jeremiah 17:5-8

Trusting the Bridge

Gephyrophobia is the fear of bridges (from the Greek gephura which means "bridge".) It is an anxiety disorder when a person finds it difficult to impossible to cross a bridge. Anyone who has crossed over the Mackinaw bridge in windy or rainy conditions can't help but relate to those who have a fear of bridges! Trusting that the bridge will not fail is a big part of gephyrophobia.

In today's first reading, Jeremiah talks about trust. He does not hold back on those that trust in human beings before they trust in God. He uses some graphic imagery of what he believes will happen to those who fail to put their trust in God.

There are many times when trusting God is not an easy thing to do; especially when life seems out of control. As we wait for God to respond to our cries and our prayers, the silence can chip away at our trust until we abandon it completely. When I experience these times in my life, I know it is not a problem with God, but a problem with the bridge between me and God.

A strong bridge to God requires regular prayer, worship, and service to others. When there is a strong bridge it is much easier to trust in God who is on the other side. When the bridge is weak due to lack of prayer, worship, and service to others, it is then that trust in God is a hard thing to come by. There are some who lose the trust altogether.

When you feel like your trust in God is waning… check your bridge. Is it strong or weak? If we can put our trust in God, then we will be like the tree planted next to the water. Even in times of distress we will still produce good fruit!

Deacon Mike

Year C
Eighth Sunday in Ordinary Time
March 3, 2019

Lent

I am so Tired of Being Ordinary!

It is unusual for us to have so many weeks of Ordinary Time in between the Christmas season and Lent. This week we will celebrate Ash Wednesday and mark the beginning of our Lenten season. It is a time for us to prepare our minds and hearts for the coming of the risen Lord at Easter. It is a season focused on prayer, fasting, and giving.

Some may ask why we need a special time to focus on these things… shouldn't we be doing them all the time? Yes! Part of our Christian lives should be a constant practice of prayer, fasting, and giving, but just like our daily lives can become very familiar and ordinary our spiritual life can become familiar and ordinary and we can just go "through the motions".

Lent gives us some time to "supercharge" our spiritual practices so that we don't fall into the trap of being "just good enough". We are made for so much more than being "ordinary"! We are made to be extraordinary in our love of Jesus and love of one another. Lent gives us the time to focus on being extraordinary.

I am so tired of being ordinary… are you?

Deacon Mike

Year C
First Sunday of Lent
March 19, 2019

Psalm 91:1-2, 10-15.

You're in Trouble Now!

When my sister and I were growing up we would egg each other on to the point where one of us would get ***the*** *look* from mom or dad. You know… the look that let you know immediately that you had crossed a line. Whoever received *the look* was usually serenaded by the other with the phrase, "You're in trouble now!" Anyone that grew up with siblings can probably relate to this scenario.

As we grow older the hope is that we avoid those things that get us into trouble. Even though we try hard to avoid being in trouble, it still happens from time to time. It may be trouble at work, or trouble at home, or trouble with a close friend. There are times when the trouble seems so overwhelming that we cannot see our way out. This is the kind of trouble that the psalmist is singing about when they say, "Be with me, Lord, when I am in trouble."

One of the three main tenets of Lent is prayer. If there is trouble in your life, Lent is a great time to deepen your prayer life and reach out to God for guidance. Trouble happens. It happens to me, to you, and to everyone else. The question is how do we respond? Do we rely only on ourselves or do we reach out in prayer and say, "Be with me, Lord"?

Deacon Mike

Year C
Second Sunday of Lent
March 17, 2019

Philippians 3:17 - 4:1

Being Occupied with Earthly Things

Most everyone experiences a time in their life when they feel like they are just hanging on and trying to get through to better times. It may be a busy schedule, it may be an illness or death in the family, it may be dealing with aging parents, or parents dealing with young children. Fr. Jude is probably feeling overwhelmed with coming to the United States and having to learn all kinds of new things about our parish and the city of Appleton! The point is that there are times when our thoughts and our energies seem totally focused on everyday life. It just happens.

In the reading from Paul to the Philippians, he talks about those who are occupied with "earthly things" versus those who are called to focus on the things of heaven. The season of Lent is a great time to check in with ourselves to see if we are so focused on the "things" of life that we are missing out on what God may be wanting to give to us to aid us on our journey to heaven. Spending some extra time in prayer and meditation will not change our circumstances, but it has the power to change us and how we deal with the "things" of life.

Finally, I would like to welcome Fr. Jude to our parish family! We can rejoice that the Lord has chosen to send Fr. Jude to us to help lead us in our Lenten journey and our journey towards our "citizenship" in heaven!

Deacon Mike

Year C
Third Sunday of Lent
March 24, 2019

Exodus 3:1-8a, 13-15

We All Have Our Meribah and Massah

In our first reading today, we hear about the Israelites grumbling against God for leading them out into the desert. This was not the last time that they would grumble against God! When we talked about this in our last RCIA session, one of the participants said, "How could they get mad after seeing the great things God did to lead them out of Egypt?" That is a good question! After experiencing the Passover and being led through the Red Sea how could the Israelites not believe that God was there to take care of them?

Then I thought of myself and how many times I grumble when things don't go the way that I think that they should even though I know that God is working in my life. Just being called to know Him and his Son is a great blessing! Being called to be a part of this parish is another blessing! But I don't think that I am alone in complaining when my plans seem to get thwarted. We all have our Meribah and Massah. Those places in our life when we ask, "Is the Lord in our midst or not?"

Lent gives us a chance to examine those times when we grumble against God (and others.) It is not always easy to see God working in our life, so we have to work to make sure we do not harden our hearts towards him. We can probably all take the advice to grumble less and trust more!

Deacon Mike

Year C/A
Fourth Sunday of Lent
March 31, 2019

1 Samuel 16:1b, 6-7, 10-13a

The Lord Looks into the Heart

I've done it. I'm sure you have done it too. We see someone or meet someone, and we make a judgment about who they are even though we really don't know them. We know the old adage, "don't judge a book by its cover" is much easier to agree with than it is to put into practice. It is part of human nature to assess others before interacting with them. It becomes a problem, however, when we act on our assumptions before we really get to know the other person. We can inflict much harm by the way we treat others based on our impressions.

In the reading from Samuel today, we hear about the anointing o David. Jesse presents his sons to Samuel one after another based on what he thinks Samuel is looking for. Jesse is presenting based on human qualities, but Samuel rejects them all… they are not chosen. Samuel tells Jesse that, *man sees the appearance, but the LORD looks into the heart*. I think there is a lesson here that we can apply to our Lenten journey.

Lent gives us an opportunity to set aside our ways of viewing others and try to see how God sees others… to put on the eyes of Christ. To Jesus, every single person is a child of God. Some have had easy paths and others have walked rough paths in their journey of life, but they are all equal in God's eyes. It is not easy for us to do especially when others are acting in a way that is not in line with the gospel. But we always need to try and remember that God sees much differently than we do because God looks into the *heart*. With our remaining time in Lent, let us all try and find something good in those we meet. It is then that we too can begin to look into the heart of others… and ourselves.

Deacon Mike

Year C/A
Fifth Sunday of Lent
April 7, 2019

John 11:1-45

Come Out!

Death is an emotional event. The passing of someone we know rarely goes without feelings of loss knowing that we will not see that person again. In today's gospel, we hear of Jesus weeping and being perturbed at the tomb of Lazarus. This gospel shows the humanity of Jesus because he is vulnerable to the same emotional reactions that we all have encountered. But the message is not about death, but about life… life in the Spirit.

When Jesus calls out to Lazarus, "Come Out!" He is not only speaking to Lazarus, but to all of us. He is calling us to come out of our isolation, he is calling us to come out of our loneliness, he is calling us to come out of our sinfulness and live a new life in the Spirit!

Lent is a season of reflection and penance. It is easy to get so focused on our shortcomings that we forget that the reason we take time to examine ourselves is so we are ready to burst forth with new life at Easter! As Paul reminds us in his letter to the Romans, if we live simply satisfying our earthly desires, we miss that we called to live life with the Spirit of God.

Let's take these last several days of Lent to take Jesus' message to heart and be ready to "Come Out!"

Deacon Mike

Year C
Palm Sunday
April 14, 2019

Holy Week

Real Time

Sunday marks the beginning of Holy Week. A time when the Church goes "all-in" for the paschal mystery in proclaiming Jesus' life, death, and resurrection. It is a week that is filled with liturgy that overflows with symbolism to help us, not just to remember, but to **re-live** the journey of Jesus in his final days and his resurrection at Easter.

Throughout the year the scriptures jump around in the life of Jesus. He is a baby in swaddling clothes, he is changing water into wine, he is healing the blind, he is preaching on a mountain, he is walking on water. All of these stories put Jesus in a new time and new place.

But not this week.

This week, we live in *real time* in the life of Jesus. We begin in Jerusalem and we end in Jerusalem. We begin at the Passover and we end a few days later. The stories that we hear are in real time… from the Last Supper on Thursday, through Jesus' crucifixion on Friday, and his resurrection on Sunday.

Come, sit at the feet of Jesus at the Last Supper. Come, stand beside Peter in the courtyard by the fire. Come, spend time at the tomb of Jesus. Come, rejoice with the apostles when it is discovered that Jesus lives! Come, live in real time.

Deacon Mike

Year C
Second Sunday of Easter
April 28, 2019

Build Well!

I don't know about you, but I am still haunted by the images of the Notre Dame cathedral engulfed in flames. As I watched the video of the catastrophe, I was moved beyond just watching a piece of history being destroyed. Through studying Church history, I know how important the French people were in restoring Christianity after the fall of Rome. The first thing I thought of when I saw the fire is how it represents the current decline of Christianity in the West.

Just as we take buildings for granted, we can also take our faith for granted.

I was heartened to see such outpouring of support and donations to rebuild even before the flames were entirely snuffed out. Perhaps this disaster will call the faithful to rebuild their own faith lives right along with the rebuilding efforts in Paris. This reflection helps me to find new meaning in our responsorial psalm today, "The stone which the builders rejected has become the cornerstone. By the LORD has this been done; it is wonderful in our eyes."

Whether it is a construction of building or of our faith life, we need to select our materials wisely and build on a solid foundation. This Easter season let us build our faith well and begin with the cornerstone that is the risen Lord!

Easter Blessings,
Deacon Mike

Year C
Third Sunday of Easter
May 5, 2019

Psalm 30:2, 4 - 6, 11 - 12, 13

With the Dawn… Rejoicing!

Bad days happen. We don't want them to happen, but they do anyway. Maybe circumstances are not what we would like. Maybe we are experiencing a loss of a friend, relative, or pet. Maybe someone we trusted did something to abuse that trust. Maybe we aren't rested, or maybe we are not feeling well. The list could get quite extensive! The point is that there are very few who are immune to the occasional (or maybe not so occasional) bad day.

Our psalmist today seems to understand that life is not always as smooth as we would like it to be, "At nightfall, weeping enters in, but with the dawn, rejoicing." It is an acknowledgment that life gets hard sometimes, but that in the Creator's great design we have the chance to start new each and every day.

So, when life gets hard try to cultivate the practice of acknowledging that even though things seem bleak, they will get better. Jesus spent a night in the garden in deep sorrow and grief, so he knows what a bad day is all about. We have a savior that understands what it feels like to be abandoned so reach out to him when bad days happen. Remember, the cross was only temporary for him… it is only temporary for you as well!

Deacon Mike

Year C
Fourth Sunday of Easter
May 12, 2019

Mother's Day

Our Common Bond

So much of what pervades our society has the tendency to accentuate what makes us different from others. Men/women, citizen/immigrant, conservative/liberal, baby-boomer/millennial, executive/homeless… well, you get the point. This list could grow quite large! And focusing on our differences usually increases our anxiety and impacts how we interact with others. But today we have a reason to celebrate one of our common bonds.

No matter our nationality, our skin color, our gender, or any other characteristic, each and every one of us has a mother. We may not have had the chance to know them or maybe only for a short while, but we all have a mother!

So today should be a day when, along with giving thanks to our mothers and those that have been mothers to us, we should also look at others and know that we all have something in common. It is our chance to see others for what characteristics we share instead of what makes us different. In the words of mothers everywhere, it is our chance to "be nice!"

Happy Mother's Day!

Deacon Mike

Year C
Fifth Sunday of Easter
May 19, 2019

Revelation 21:1-5a

Making Things New

I love being able to spend time in my workshop. It is the time that I can put aside the busyness of life and lose myself in drawing, shaping, and creating. There is something very rewarding about envisioning a project and watch it come to fruition. Lisa calls my workshop my "happy place."

Along with creating and building, one of things that I like to do is to restore old pieces of furniture. It is different than creating from scratch because you never know what lies beneath the unsightly surface and hours of work could end up being wasted if the wood is bad underneath. But it can also be awesome to see beautiful craftsmanship come back to life by making it new again!

In our second reading today, John shares with us his vision where at the end of time the Lamb of God sits on the throne and makes all things new. The thought of this should bring us great joy! No matter what we have been through or what we have done, Jesus will strip away all the grime, all the scars, and all the hurt and we will be made new again!

We can do this too.

We can make things new when we care for those that have had a rough life or are going through a tough time. We can make things new when we set aside our cares for a while and are there for others. We can make all things new by listening to someone else's story to help them strip away that which hides their true beauty! Come, let us make all things new!

Deacon Mike

Year C
Sixth Sunday of Easter
May 26, 2019

Psalm 67:2 - 3, 5 - 6, 8

Let it Shine!

Most of us are familiar with the story of Moses leading the
Israelites out of captivity in Egypt and their journey through the
desert. Part of that story is when Moses goes up on the
mountain and God passes in front of him and he is only allowed
to see his back (for no one can see the face of God and live.)
After this encounter, Moses becomes so bright in appearance
that the Israelites thought they were seeing a ghost! In our
responsorial psalm today, the psalmist sings, "May God have
pity on us and bless us; may he let his face shine upon us."

What happens if we let God shine his face upon us?

Like Moses, we are transformed. We may not become so bright
that others think they are encountering a ghost! But our outward
appearance does change because we smile more, laugh more,
and carry with us the joy of the creator. We are transformed on
the inside too. We encourage others, we help others, and we are
joyful even when things are not the best.

Right about now you are probably thinking… this is all fine, but
when to we get to see God? The answer is we only need to look!
If we look for God in creation, we will find him. If we look for God
in the face of others, we will find him. If we look for God in the
goodness of others, we will find him. We need only to open our
heart to let God's face shine upon us!

In a special way this weekend we can find the face of God in
those that sacrificed so much in service to our country. Let us all
take time to remember and thank those that served so that we
can live in the freedom to seek the face of God without fear.

Deacon Mike

Year C
The Ascension of the Lord
June 2, 2019

Luke 24:46-53

Are You Ready?

Most people who have started work at a new company know that there is a certain period of time called the "honeymoon phase" where everyone you meet is all smiles and willing to help out in an instant. There are also many who know what it is like when the honeymoon phase is over! Once you are trained, you are expected to do your job and those that we so friendly in the beginning and willing to help are nowhere to be found. I think that most of us have experienced this at one time or another!

We have spent the last six weeks basking in the glow of the Easter resurrection. It is the "honeymoon phase" of our liturgical calendar. The discipline of Lent is behind us and we live in the joy of the risen Jesus. We celebrate baptisms, first Eucharists, and confirmations and everyone seems happy!

Today we celebrate the Ascension of the Lord. We hear of the disciples being with Jesus as he is taken up to heaven and then returning to Jerusalem with great joy! But I can picture them sitting all together the next day looking at each other waiting to hear someone say what happens next. They are unaware that soon the Holy Spirit will be given to them and they will go out preaching to the ends of the earth! We know that we are called to do the same…

Are you ready?

Deacon Mike

Year C
Pentecost Sunday
June 9, 2019

Is it Getting Hot in Here?

For several decades the policy of the National Forest Service
was to extinguish any fire no matter what the origin. While the
intention was well meaning, it came with some unintended
consequences. The first consequence is that without burning
every so often, the forest floor would build up with all kinds of
brush and then when fires broke out, they were super intense
and very hard to control. Another consequence is that there were
no new sequoia trees growing in California. As was discovered
later, sequoias need fire to reproduce! The heat from the fire
opens the cones to release the seeds inside. But the fire also
burns the leafy canopy so more sunlight can hit the forest floor,
and it burns away all the debris so the seeds can make it into the
ground. What man saw as harmful; nature saw as necessary.

Today we hear about the Holy Spirit coming upon the apostles
like "tongues of fire" and they came alive and started to proclaim
in different languages so that all present could understand.
Without the fire, the apostles were much like cones from the
sequoias… full of life-giving seeds without any way of releasing
them.

It can be the same for us also. Sometimes we need a little fire…
a little heat in our lives to release the Holy Spirit inside of us.
Most of us avoid the heat so that we don't ever have to worry
about getting burned, but much like the forest, we need some
flames every once in a while, to clear out the brush and
brambles that can gather in our lives.

So, this Pentecost, think about stepping outside of your comfort
zone. Volunteer more, join a study group or Alpha, or try a new
ministry at church. Each of us knows what holds us back from
letting the Spirit have more room in our life. Maybe it's time turn
up the heat!

What's that sizzling sound I hear?

Deacon Mike

Year C
Most Holy Trinity
June 16, 2019

Romans 5:1-5

Where are the Ear Plugs?

I have been blessed to have music be a part of my life. All through elementary school, Mrs. Kurtz would show us all kinds of different instruments and engage us in activities that made learning music fun and exciting. Middle school is when it was time to pick an instrument to play in the band. My choice was the French Horn. I loved the warm tones that the French Horn resonates and even though I was warned that it is one of the more difficult instruments to play, I was dedicated to trying. Bruised lips, squeaks and squanks were common starting out, but over the course of a few years, my skill began to improve. I haven't played the French Horn since high school, some &# years ago, but I am thankful that I did because it taught me that some things only happen with time and practice.

In Paul's letter to the Corinthians today, he talks about we arrive at hope. He says that we have hope through afflictions and as we move through those afflictions, we gain endurance. Over the course of time, we come to realize that even though we have hardships we learn to live through them with hope in Jesus. Hope comes through enduring trials and once we live in hope there is no trial that cannot be overcome.

Nobody wants to live through afflictions and we certainly do not need to seek them out just to have hope! But when trials do enter our lives, we can bear them grudgingly or we can work on building our endurance and character. It is not an easy thing to do, but with time and practice, we can live in the hope that Father, Son, and Spirit provide!

Deacon Mike

Year C
Corpus Christi
June 23, 2019

Genesis 14:18-20 and Luke 9:11b-17

Melchize-who?

In our first reading today, Abram (who would later become Abraham) meets up with a priest named Melchizedek after returning from a victorious battle. Although not much is known about Melchizedek, we do know that he is not one of the normal "Levite" priests of Israel. His name suggests that he has a priesthood that is his own that has no beginning or no end. That is one of the reasons why Paul compares Jesus' priesthood to Melchizedek.

In the story, notice that Melchizedek brings out bread and wine (gifts) to Abram. This is backwards of what happens with the Levitical priests because they are *given* the gifts as part of their priestly service. For his gesture, Abram is abundant with his gifts to Melchizedek.

In the gospel, we see that Jesus is the one ministering to the crowds. Really, it is *he* who should be given a portion from those listening to him. Instead, he blesses those that are there with food that is so generous it is overflowing at the end. All this is somewhat interesting but… so what?

When we bless others by giving of ourselves and of our treasures regardless of what we think is "rightfully" ours, everyone will be abundantly blessed. This is at the heart of stewardship, recognizing that what we have is a gift and when we share that gift, we are blessed. So, as we go about our busy summer activities, let us resist the temptation to "take a break" from living out our faith and let us bless those who cross our paths regardless of their status in life.

Melchizedeacon Mike

Year C
Thirteenth Sunday in Ordinary Time
June 30, 2019

Galatians 5:1, 13-18

The Other Freedom

This week our country will celebrate our independence. Many will
relish having the day off work to travel, camp, or go on an outing.
There are others who will mark the day more solemnly knowing
they have lost friends or family in the effort to keep the freedoms
that we have as citizens of the United States. Whether we see
the fourth of July as a day of leisure or a day of remembrance,
we should all remember the old axiom… freedom isn't free.

In Paul's letter to the Galatians, he talks about a different kind of
freedom… freedom in the Spirit. He encourages the Galatians
not to waste the gift of this freedom by living the same way they
used to live, but to put their freedom to use by serving their
sisters and brothers. The cost of having the freedom to live in the
Spirit is that we work at giving up the things in our life that run
contrary to the gospel… freedom isn't free.

In the end, however, we should always remember that what we
gain by living in the Spirit is far greater than the cost of what we
surrender. The earthly things that we give up are not really
freedoms, but yokes in disguise. Just as Paul encourages the
Galatians to not put on the yoke of slavery under the Jewish law,
we must be careful not to slip into the yoke of slavery of earthy
vices. We must try our best to live in the freedom of the Spirit…
freedom isn't free.

Deacon Mike

Year C
Fourteenth Sunday in Ordinary Time
July 7, 2019

Luke 10:1-12, 17-20

Well That's Just Rude!

I recently read an article that said that people who engage strangers in conversation tend to live longer lives. I emailed the article to my mom with the note, "You'll live to be 102!" My mom is always engaging others in conversation whether she knows them or not. She has grown many relationships over the years through her willingness to talk to others. This is just who my mom is! Having this as an example makes part of today's gospel message a little baffling. As Jesus sends out the disciples in pairs, he tells them to greet no one on their way.

Wait a minute! Isn't evangelization all about engaging others!?

The short answer is yes. But Jesus isn't telling the disciples to avoid others, only that they need to remain focused on their mission. He knows that if they spend their time visiting with everyone they meet on their travels; they will be taking away from the time needed to fulfill the task at hand. It is the same with us.

On our faith journey, it is important to avoid distractions that keep us from our mission. It probably has nothing to do with avoiding others, but it could have a lot to do with other distractions in our life. Are we distracted by social media, sports, or spending habits to the point of hurting our relationship with God and with others? Do we engage others so that we can eventually share the joy of the gospel or do we leave it up to someone else? Focus on the mission and you cannot go wrong!

If you see my mom visiting, make sure to say hi!

Deacon Mike

Year C
Fifteenth Sunday in Ordinary Time
July 14, 2019

Deuteronomy 30:10-14

Just Do It!

One of the most successful advertising slogans in history is the phrase "Just Do It." It was first used by Nike over thirty years ago but there are few people that do not know where "Just Do It" came from. It is a clear, concise message to fitness buffs to stop making excuses and get out there and get it done!

Moses has a very similar message to the Israelites in our first reading today. He is speaking to them about the commandments set before them and how they are not mysterious, they are not beyond reach, and they are not far away. As a matter of fact, they are already in the heart, they just need to be carried out... in other words, "Just do it!"

There are times in our faith life when we may feel a dryness in our prayer life or maybe feel like our effort to reach out to others are falling short or not appreciated. It is during those times when we can feel farthest away from God, but sometimes we just need to persevere knowing that God's promises are not mysterious, not far away, and not beyond reach. We just need to keep the faith and "Just Do It!"

Deacon Mike

Year C
Sixteenth Sunday in Ordinary Time
July 21, 2019

Luke 10:38-42

Choose the Better Part

Our gospel today is the familiar story of Martha and her sister
Mary. While Mary is busy making sure everything gets done, she
complains that her sister is just sitting around listening to Jesus. I
always feel sorry for Martha when Jesus kind of rebukes her by
saying the Mary has chosen the better part. I mean, let's be
serious, if everyone just sat around at the feet of Jesus nothing
would get done! But there is something more to this story then
just saying it is better to listen to Jesus than to be busy all the
time. It's about choosing. In this circumstance, Mary chose the
better part.

Something that we could take away from this reading is to ask
ourselves if we are in the habit of choosing the better part? Do
we choose the better part when get into arguments with family
members or co-workers? Do we choose the better part when
talking with others turns into gossip that is none of our business?
Do we choose the better part when those we are with want to do
things that run contrary to our faith? Do we choose the better
part when we are around those less fortunate than ourselves?

Part of living the life of a Christian is learning to choose the
better part in every aspect of our lives… at home, at work, at
worship, and at play. It usually doesn't happen all at once but is
something that we need to do over and over again. Even if we
slip now and then we need to work to choose the better part the
next time.

Should you read this article again?

Choose the better part!

Deacon Mike

Year C
Seventeenth Sunday in Ordinary Time
July 28, 2019

Genesis 18:20-32

Bargaining with God

Our first reading today has Abraham playing the part of a reverse auctioneer trying to save the towns of Sodom and Gomorrah. When I hear this reading, I tend to get lost in Abraham's method of bargaining: fifty, forty-five, forty, thirty, twenty, ten. Come on already... just ask for the ten! But by focusing in on the process, I miss out that this story has a real human element to it because this is how many of us go to God in supplication (asking for things.) We tend to dance around the edges of our requests wondering (much like Abraham) what we can ask of God without overstepping our bounds. Can I ask God for the perfect house, the perfect job, the perfect relationship or am I not worthy of having the best?

In the Gospel today, Jesus talks to his disciples about prayer. He gives them His prayer and then goes on to say that persistence in prayer is important, that those who seek will receive, and the best request we can make of God is to ask for the Holy Spirit. Say what?! At the end of today's gospel, Jesus says that God is there to give the Holy Spirit to those that ask him. So, what does the Holy Spirit have to do with a house, job, or relationship?

The gifts of the Holy Spirit are wisdom, understanding, counsel, fortitude, knowledge, piety, and fear (awe) of the Lord. When we ask for the gifts of the Holy Spirit, we ask to have the gifts needed to discern what we need for our lives so that when we go to God with our supplications we don't have to wonder about dancing around the edges... we have the wisdom, understanding, and knowledge to request what we *really* need for our lives. Go to God always in prayer, but at the end ask for the Holy Spirit and see what happens in your life!

Deacon Mike

Year C
Eighteenth Sunday in Ordinary Time
August 4, 2019

Ecclesiastes 1:2; 2:21-23

This Article is Vanity

"Vanity of vanities, says Qoheleth, vanity of vanities! All things are vanity!"

Kind of makes you wonder if Qoheleth was a carpenter that had to install one too many bathroom cabinets!

While it is easy to dismiss Qoheleth in what seems to be a very pessimistic view of life, we can miss out on what he really was trying to say… focus on the things that are important. As the book of Ecclesiastes continues, Qoheleth goes on and on about how man's existence on earth really doesn't amount to much. But what he realizes in the end is that our only concern is the things of God. At the end of Ecclesiastes, this is what is written: "The last word, when all is heard: Fear God and keep his commandments, for this concerns all humankind."

Quoheleth should remind all of us that we need to step back from time to time and see what vanities exist in our life. Are we working just to pay for "stuff", or do we practice good stewardship with our resources? Do we spend too much time doing things that may be fun, but basically amount to time-killers or do we spend time helping others? What other things in our life may be vanity?

Does anyone know a good plumber?

Deacon Mike

Year C
Nineteenth Sunday in Ordinary Time
August 11, 2019

Luke 12:32-48

Being Ready

Almost every family has one. Some families have more than one
Yes… I am talking about that person who seems to never be on
time! You know them. They are your spouse, children, parents,
or friends. They are the bane of those relish in promptness and
have been known to cause the tearing of garments and the
grinding of teeth! They are loved, yet they can bring such angst
as to render others speechless!

All kidding aside… in today's gospel Jesus talks about the need
to be ready and uses some striking examples to make his point.
Even after Jesus was taken to heaven, his followers often wrote
about staying vigilant and being ready. What is so important
about the need to be ready?

What Jesus and his followers knew is that if we live our lives as if
Jesus was coming tomorrow, we would never have to worry
about not being invited into his kingdom. Being ready is about
making the choice to follow Jesus and then living out what he
taught. This is not an easy thing to do. Jesus knows this as he
says at the end of today's gospel that much will be required of
those that have much and even more will be required of those
that have more. In other words, we cannot rest on our laurels,
there is always more to do. As followers of Jesus, we are the
ones who have been given much so much is required of us. So
let us all be ready for Jesus!

Patiently waiting,
Deacon Mike

Year C
Twentieth Sunday in Ordinary Time
August 18, 2019

Diaconate

Deacons – what are they all about?

Most parishioners see a deacon serving at mass but may have little contact otherwise. I thought I would take this week's musings to talk about deacons, who they are and what they do.

Deacons are men who feel called to serve others. The root word for deacon comes from the Greek *diakonia* that translates to "service" so a deacon by title is someone who serves others through the Church. Since ordination is a life-long commitment, there is a minimum of five years of formation before someone is ordained to the diaconate (the order of deacons.) Once accepted for formation, candidates study a wide range of topics such as scripture, spirituality, prayer, pastoral care, and the "nuts and bolts" needed to perform their assigned tasks.

There are three areas that deacons are ordained into: service of the word, service of the altar, and service of charity. Service of word is visible in the deacon reading the gospel and giving homilies. Service of the altar is seen by the deacon assisting the priest at mass and are stewards of the cup (that is why deacons are ministers of the blood of Christ instead of the body of Christ at mass.) But the bulk of the deacon's work usually goes unseen through their service of charity. Deacons serve in a wide range of charitable work which can be as unique as each deacon! Most deacons have a full-time "secular" job, so they have "one foot in the world and the other foot in the Church."

Deacons are ordained to service to the bishop of the diocese but are assigned to a specific parish to assist the pastor in the needs of the parish community. Deacons can baptize, officiate at weddings, preside at funerals outside of mass, and lead liturgies with communion outside of mass along with helping in a variety of areas in the Church.

Although this is a brief sketch of the deacon, I hope that maybe you learned something new! And for those of you who find this intriguing and want to learn more… let's talk!

Servant Mike

Year C
Twenty-first Sunday in Ordinary Time
August 25, 2019

Hebrews 12:5-7, 11-13

Weak Knees

Yes, I am at that age when instead of referring to my knees as "right" and "left" I refer to them as the "good knee" and the "bad knee." No complaints… I have had some great adventures on those knees, and I am not done yet! In today's second reading, when the author exhorts the reader to "strengthen your drooping hands and your weak knees," they are probably not referring to the same thing as me!

The weak knees that the author is talking about are the weak knees we get when we are corrected for not doing what we are supposed to be doing. I had this happen recently when I had to submit my preliminary thesis proposal to my class where it was quite quickly ripped to shreds. Ouch. But because of the criticism that my classmates provided, I was able to go back to the drawing board and submit a proposal that was well received by the program director. If I would have become angry or defensive during the criticism of the first proposal, I would have lost the insights that I needed to produce a proposal that is ready for submission to the thesis committee. I had to strengthen my weak knees.

The second reading reminds us that when we are corrected in our faith life, instead of sitting around and pouting about it, we need to strengthen our resolve and use the experience to strengthen our faith. The author even says that we should be glad to be corrected because it means that we are loved. Remember, the opposite of love is not hate; it is indifference. People will generally not correct those they do not care about, so count it as joy when someone takes the time to point out things in our life that maybe we need to examine more closely especially when it comes to faith!

Excuse me, I need to sit down.

Deacon Mike

Year C
Twenty-second Sunday in Ordinary Time
September 1, 2019

Luke 14:1, 7-14

Dining with Pharisees on Labor Day

On Monday we celebrate the efforts of all workers to the well-being of our society. It is a day that has been traditionally marked with parades, sports, travelling, and outings. It is also the time when many parents cannot help but crack a small smile knowing that the kids will be in full swing at school and the household regains some normalcy! The recognition of the efforts of workers to our society is a good thing. It is also something that should be put into context.

In the gospel today, Jesus is at the home of one of pharisees for a meal. As he observes people jostling for positions of honor at the table, he tells a story that reminds the listener to be careful about how much they exalt themselves lest someone with more prominence removes them from their place (with much embarrassment.) If we apply this to our work, then we should be more concerned with the contribution we make than with the recognition we receive.

Labor comes in a huge array of endeavors and is not limited to what we do "at a job." Some of the most important labor we do happens close to home. It is in the laundry we do, the dishes we clean, the yard we mow, and the countless other tasks we do for the betterment of our families. These labors probably don't get the recognition they deserve. But if we go back to the gospel, these are the kind of labors that, when done out of love, will have Jesus say to us, "my friend, move to a higher position at my table." Let us all be humble in what we do.

Happy Labor Day!
Deacon Mike

Year C
Twenty-third Sunday in Ordinary Time
September 8, 2019

Lk 14:25-33

Counting the Cost

One of my favorite movies is *Moneyball*. It is the real-life story of
Billy Beane who was the general manager of the Oakland A's
baseball team in the early 2000's. Billy hired Peter Brand and the
two of them re-wrote how baseball clubs hired players. Instead of
relying on the instincts of their scouts, they hired based on actual
statistics of the players. In the first year of their new system, the
team won 20 consecutive games and the finished first place in
their division. The movie does a good job of showing how Billy
and Peter were able to build a winning team around lesser-
known players by knowing the value that each player could bring
to the team. They excelled at knowing the cost.

In the gospel today, Jesus uses the example of someone
wanting to build a tower. He questions who would start building
unless they knew they had the resources to finish what they
started. Jesus is asking the crowd if they know the cost of
following him before they start their journey.

What about us? If we truly want to follow Jesus it should cost us
our resentfulness, our anger, our jealousy, our selfishness, our
gossiping, and our pride, just to name a few. Do we ever think
about the cost of following Jesus? The cost is real, but it is
nothing compared to the treasure that awaits those that are
willing to pay the price.

Anyone have a calculator handy?

Deacon Mike

Year C
Twenty-fourth Sunday in Ordinary Time
September 15, 2019

Exodus 32:7-11, 13-14

Loosen Up!

One of the daily routines at our house is the competition for floor space in the living room to stretch out before going to bed. Lisa and I know that if we do not work to stay limber our muscles will continue to get stiffer until it becomes difficult to move. We will be stuck.

In the reading from Exodus today, the Lord instructs Moses to address the Israelites who have turned back to worshipping other Gods. He calls them "stiff-necked" because they keep falling back into old habits. They fail to see that God is the God of new birth in the Spirit. They are stuck.

Every one of us needs to be on guard about becoming stuck in our spiritual life. We always need to look for ways of stretching ourselves a little past our comfort zone so that we do not become stiff in our ways. Fortunately, St. Bernard's has just the thing!

Discipleship Nights!

If you have not experienced discipleship nights, you are missing out on something special. A great meal with exceptional fellowship is followed with some worship time. After that, the children and youth go to faith formation and the adults have two programs to choose from, either **Alpha** or a series on the **Eucharist**. It does not matter if you are new to the faith or have been Catholic for decades… our parish needs your involvement to make Discipleship Nights successful.

Here are my suggestions:
If you want to grow in your relationship with God and others, try Alpha. Put away your preconceived ideas about what Alpha is or isn't and come experience it for yourself. And yes… we need those that are experienced in their faith to share with others.

If you want to learn more about the Catholic Faith, then come to the series on the Eucharist. Don't assume you know everything there is to know about the summit of our Faith!

Small groups not your style? Then why not help cook, serve, or clean up? This is a great way of giving back to the St. Bernard community so others can grow in their faith! And who knows, you might make a new friend or two!

Discipleship nights kick off at 5:30 in the parish hall on September 25th. Bring your appetite for food, fellowship, and spiritual growth and get ready to loosen up!

Deacon Mike

Year C
Twenty-fifth Sunday in Ordinary Time
September 22, 2019

Amos 8:4-7

Whew, I'm Glad That's Over!

I am as guilty as anyone else. There are times when I view going
to Mass as something that I have to "fit into my schedule." Don't
get me wrong… going to Mass no matter what is happening is
better than not going at all, but Mass needs to be something
more than just another activity in our lives. We need to enter into
the Mass with hearts and minds ready to hear the word of God
and to be in communion with God and others as we celebrate
the Eucharist. We should always go to Mass ready to be
changed.

In our first reading today, Amos is admonishing the crowds
because they are anxious to have the time of worship be done
so they can go back to what they were doing before. "When is
the Sabbath over that we may display the wheat?" They are
failing to be changed in their relationship with God and with
others… especially the needy.

Most everyone I know has a busy schedule. The demands of
work and family leave very little time for relaxation and being
able to appreciate the beauty that God has created for us. But in
order to appreciate the gifts that God has given to us, we need to
try and make our time in worship as beneficial as possible. One
of the ways that I have found to enter more deeply into Mass is
to go over the readings beforehand so that when I hear them
proclaimed at Mass, I am more open to being changed than just
trying to pay attention to the words. I encourage everyone to find
ways of making Mass something more than just another thing
that has to be fit into the schedule.

Be willing to be changed.

Deacon Mike

Year C
Twenty-sixth Sunday in Ordinary Time
September 29, 2019

1 Timothy 6:11-16

A Noble Confession

My favorite author is Steven Lawhead. One of the elements that
draws me to his writing is that many of his stories center around
a person who most would consider ordinary. As the stories
progress, the main character slowly develops the qualities
he/she needs to rise to the challenge. It reminds me of the
saying that God does not call the qualified, he qualifies those he
calls!

In the second reading today, Paul reminds Timothy of the noble
confession he made before many witnesses and links it to the
noble confession Jesus made in front of Pontius Pilate. He is
exhorting Timothy to proclaim his faith and receive the rewards
of eternal life. It seems to me like Paul is telling Timothy he has
what it takes, he just needs to put it into practice.

When I look out in the congregation at Mass, I see many people
with wonderful qualities and gifts. Some use their gifts in service
of the church by helping to teach others, be companions, or help
with those less fortunate. There are others that I hope are using
their gifts in settings that I do not see.

What about us? Do we live a life that shows others how
important Jesus is to us? Are we able to make our "noble
confession" by living out our faith or do we need to work on
developing qualities that will help us bring Jesus to others? As
Paul says to Timothy, pursue righteousness, devotion, faith,
love, patience, and gentleness and see what a great disciple you
can become!

Still working on it,

Deacon Mike

Year C
Twenty-seventh Sunday in Ordinary Time
October 6, 2019

2 Timothy 1:6-8, 13-14

Follow the Yellow Brick Road

I am sure most everyone has seen the movie *The Wizard of Oz.* The tale of four misfits on their journey to the magical land of Oz where they search for the wizard to give them the one thing that will make their lives complete.

One of the characters is the cowardly lion. He is a misfit because lions are supposed to be the king of the jungle and fearless. But this poor lion is afraid of just about everything and it gets in the way of him being able to help his companions on their journey. Instead of leading the way and confronting obstacles, his friends have to use their energy to keep dragging him along which slows down their travels.

Our second reading talks about being cowardly. In Paul's letter, he tells Timothy that God did not give him a spirit of cowardice, but a spirit of love and self-control. Paul knows that if Timothy is going to be a witness for Jesus that he cannot be cowardly but needs to be confident of himself and his mission.

 What about us? Are we confident in our ability to bring others to Jesus or do we let our cowardice get in the way? Do we convince ourselves that we are not smart enough or holy enough to be a good witness and miss opportunities to share Jesus with others? Remember, God gave us all a spirit of love and we need to be confident that he wants each of us to share that good news with others!

Roar for Jesus!

Deacon Mike

Year C
Twenty-eighth Sunday in Ordinary Time
October 13, 2019

2 Kings 5:14-17

Sacred Places

Recently Lisa and I took a long weekend to head up to the Upper
Peninsula to visit some of our favorite spots. We love to travel
there in the fall when the forests are ablaze with color and the
wildlife is active foraging for supplies for the upcoming winter.
We also enjoy the quietness that seems to descend on the area
as the busy summer season fades away and the locals make
their own preparations for the months ahead. These trips refresh
my soul.

In today's first reading, Naaman has such a profound experience
in Israel that he begs the prophet Elisha to be able to take some
of the earth from Israel so that he can worship on that ground.
The place has become special to Naaman because he was
cured of his leprosy that it has become sacred. His soul has
been refreshed.

What are some of the places that are sacred in our lives? What
makes them so special? Is St. Bernard one of those places?

Our parish should be one of those places that we view as a
sacred space. It is a place where we come to encounter Jesus
and our friends and family. It is a place where we come to hear
the word of God and come face-to-face with Jesus in the
Eucharist. It is a place where each one of us has been called to
be at this moment. What can we do to make St. Bernard to the
most sacred place it can be?

Excuse me, I have to unload my trailer!

Deacon Mike

Year C
Twenty-ninth Sunday in Ordinary Time
October 20, 2019

Exodus 17:8-13

What Are Friends For?

Growing up I had a group of friends that did almost everything together. And just like the cowboy had his trusted horse, each one of us had our trusted two-wheeled steed... we rode our bicycles *everywhere*.

For the most part, we were responsible enough riders, but we had one weakness… building ramps. We would scrounge around for anything that would make a good ramp, and when we would build a really good one, we would make a few practice runs to mark how far we could jump and then we would lay down next to the ramp like logs while one of us would speed towards the ramp making the jump. A tremendous amount of trust was needed to be laying underneath that ramp!

In the reading from Exodus today, we hear the story of Aaron and Hur holding up the arms of Moses so that Joshua could win the battle below. Moses trusts that Aaron and Hur will not desert him in his time of need and they trust that God will not let them be overrun by the enemy. They do not abandon Moses or Joshua and by doing so they exhibit one of the qualities that make a great friend.

Jesus exudes this quality in his friendship with us. He is always at our side ready to support us when we do not have the strength to hold ourselves up. No matter what is happening in our lives, no matter what battle is raging, he will be by our side. As we trust Jesus to be with us no matter what… Jesus trusts that you will win the battle! There is no better friend than Jesus.

Does anyone have a card for my spokes?

Deacon Mike

Year C
Thirtieth Sunday in Ordinary Time
October 27, 2019

Sirach 35:12-14, 16-18

Go Pack Go!

Something that I have pondered from time to time is whether or not God listens to the prayers of those who pray for an outcome to a game? If so… which team and why? (I will give you a minute to think about that.) My point is that each team will likely have players, coaches, and fans praying for their team to win. It begs the question: if a team loses, were their prayers not answered?

In the first reading today, Sirach gives a list of those whose prayers will be heard by God. It is not the rich, powerful, or influential, but is the lowly, the poor, the widow, and the oppressed. Even our psalm today says that the Lord hears the cry of the poor.

This should make us a little uneasy because if God hears the cry of the poor then he knows that we may not be living up to our calling as followers of Christ. If there are poor among us, then we have work to do. Not only monetarily poor, but those who are poor in spirit, poor in health, and poor in companionship.

What do we do to help alleviate the cry of the poor? Are we kind, caring, and compassionate or do we talk about others when they are not around? Do we reach out to those we do not know, or do we wait for them to approach us? Do we take care of those closest to us in their need for support and encouragement? Do we help those less fortunate than ourselves? Do we rely on God to take care of the poor or do we realize that *we* are the ones God relies on to take care of the poor?

Gotta go… the game is on!

Deacon Mike

Year C
Thirty-first Sunday in Ordinary Time
November 3, 2019

Wisdom 11:22—12:2

God Made Frogs Too!

When I was in fourth grade, our class had the opportunity to
work with pottery. There was a local artisan who would make the
pieces of pottery and then we would paint them before they were
glazed and fired in the kiln. I remember picking out a frog with its
mouth open so you could put stuff inside. My mom used it to put
her scouring pad next to the sink. She loved that frog, not
because of its beauty (it was not the most attractive thing in the
world) but because of who made it.

Our first reading today is from the book of Wisdom. This passage
speaks beautifully of how God loves all that he created. The
writer goes on to tell how God gives each of us the chance to set
things right when we go astray so that we can be one with him.
This passage mimics the old adage, "Love the sinner, hate the
sin." I think for many of us this is easier said than done because
we lose sight of the creator of all.

So how can we work on loving those who may not live up to our
standards? I think a good place to start is to recognize the works
of God that are all around us. If we can see God's handiwork in
things that are beautiful then we learn to see the work of God in
everyone we meet. When we can start to see with the eyes of
God we can try and find the good in everyone, and when we
come to find the good in everyone, we begin to transform the
world!

Deacon Mike

Year C
Thirty-second Sunday In Ordinary Time
November 10, 2019

Psalm 17:1, 5-6, 8, 15

I Like Mine Dipped in Caramel

Every day before going to work, Lisa lovingly prepares a lunch
for each of us. One of the staples of my lunch box is an apple
because, "You know we are supposed to have seven servings of
fruit and vegetables every day!" [Insert "Yes, dear" here]. I know
that Lisa is just trying to make sure that we eat a somewhat
healthy diet so that we are able to go out and meet the day!

In our responsorial psalm today, the psalmist is petitioning God
to hear their prayer and says, "Keep me as the apple of your
eye." To keep someone as the apple of your eye means that you
keep that person firmly fixed in your mind's eye. The psalmist is
saying to God, "Keep me in your sight."

While it is always good to reach out towards God in prayer, we
also need to know that God always keeps each one of us as the
apple of his eye. This is the very first part of the Kerygma
(pronounced Ker-ig-ma) … God loves me and has created me to
be in relationship with Him. We need to come to know this and
fix it in our hearts.

So, the next time you see an apple, remember that you are loved
by God and that he keeps you as the apple of His eye. Your
existence is not by chance. You are called by God to love him
and your neighbor in this time and in this place. You are here for
a purpose in the story of salvation history!

Deacon Mike

Year C
Thirty-third Sunday in Ordinary Time
November 17, 2019

2 Thessalonians 3:7-12

One Ringy Dingy

Some of us more mature folks can remember the days of the
party line. No, it wasn't used to have a lot of people on the line
for fun, but it was that many parties shared the same line in order
to save money. If someone else was on the line you had to wait
your turn before using the phone. One of quirks of the party line
was that you could overhear other people's conversations by
listening in on them. While the vast majority of people would
never engage in such an activity, there always seemed to be one
or two people in the neighborhood that knew everybody's
business!

In Paul's letter to the Thessalonians, he says that he has heard
of some who go about minding the business of others instead of
focusing on their own work. Paul's instruction? Work quietly.
Paul knows that when we are focused on the affairs of others,
we are probably not paying attention to what needs adjustment
in our own life. It is a distraction to the whisperings of God and
can lead to many unhealthy habits.

Unfortunately, our culture not only thinks it is okay to be in
someone else's business but promotes it! I think of all the
"reality" shows that are available and how that fosters a mindset
of voyeurism that can quickly move to everyday life. It can
become natural to want to know everything that is going on.
Guess what… we don't need to know!

Our Christian faith calls us to become genuinely concerned with
others, not for our own satisfaction, but so that we can do
everything we can to help our sisters and brothers. Let us take
Paul's advice and work quietly for our salvation and for those
around us.
Could someone please answer the phone? I'm a little busy here!

Deacon Mike

Year C
Our Lord Jesus Christ, King of the Universe
November 24, 2019

2 Samuel 5:1-3 / Colossians 1:12-2 0/ Luke 23:35-43

All Good Things Must Come to an End

There are many endings in this world: books, movies, friendships, jobs, relationships, and even life itself. It seems like the better they are, the harder it is to see them end. Many times, we can sense when things are coming to an end and we try and do things to have them last just a little bit longer so we can hold on to what is bringing us happiness, comfort, joy, or love.

Today is the end of our liturgical year. Next week we celebrate the first Sunday of Advent in Year A. Unlike most endings, however, there is a great anticipation of "what's next?" We look forward to the start of Advent and a chance to prepare our hearts and minds for the coming birth of Jesus. What is old becomes new again!

The readings today challenge us to look past our earthly vision of endings to one that is focused on the Kingdom of God where there is no end. We don't need to try and hold on to what is because we live in the hope of what is to come! So, let us remember that even though there are many endings in life, Jesus has the power to help us make something new!

See you next year!

Deacon Mike

Year A
First Sunday of Advent
December 1, 2019

Liturgical Seasons

And So It Begins

Today marks the beginning of the liturgical year 2020. Since it is the beginning of a new year, I thought I would take this article to write about the different liturgical seasons in the Church.

Advent
Advent begins on the 4th Sunday before Christmas. It can range from November 27th to December 3rd. The liturgical color for Advent is violet. Advent marks a time of interior preparation for the coming of Jesus at Christmas.

Christmas
The Christmas season begins with the Vigil Masses on December 24th and goes until the Feast of the Baptism of the Lord (this year on January 12th.) The liturgical color is white. Christmas is a time of celebration of Emmanuel (God with us.)

Ordinary Time (1)
Ordinary time does not mean that it is less special! It is a translation from the Latin Ordo meaning ordered or marked time. Ordinary time begins on the Monday following the Baptism of the Lord and goes until the Tuesday proceeding Ash Wednesday. The liturgical color for ordinary time is green, but there is a spattering of different colors for feast days along the way!

Lent
Ash Wednesday marks the beginning of the Lenten Season. It is six weeks and four days before Easter. It can range from February 4th to March 11th. This year it is February 26th. The liturgical color for Lent is purple. Lent is a time of more intense inner preparation for the celebration of Easter and used as a time for prayer, fasting, and charity.

Easter
Easter is not just one day, but an entire season! It begins with the Easter Vigil and concludes at Pentecost. Easter Sunday is

the first Sunday after the first full moon after the spring equinox. It can be from March 22nd to April 25th. This year it is April 12th. The liturgical color is white. Easter is a time of celebration of the life, death, and resurrection of Jesus!

Ordinary Time (2)
The remainder of ordinary time begins the Monday after Pentecost (this year May 31st) are goes through to the Saturday before the first Sunday of Advent and we start all over again!

If you want to learn more about this year's calendar visit http://www.usccb.org/about/divine-worship/liturgical-calendar/upload/2020cal.pdf

Year A
Second Sunday of Advent
December 8, 2019

Matthew 3:1-12

There's Always One Bad Apple!

In an episode of the sitcom Seinfeld, Kramer wants Jerry to return a peach to the grocery store because it isn't any good. Jerry objects to the suggestion of returning a piece of fruit by saying that, "Fruit is a gamble… I know that going in!" Anyone who buys fruit knows how frustrating it is to find out the inside is different than what it looks like on the outside. This can be applied to people as well. There are many who can put on a good appearance on the outside and yet not be so good on the inside.

In the gospel today, John the Baptist reacts to the Pharisees and the Sadducees by saying that they should produce good fruit as evidence of their repentance. This is a challenge to them that just following the letter of the law it does not necessarily mean they are doing what they are supposed to be doing. There should be more to faith than checking off boxes.

The same is true for us. When we boil our faith life down to following rituals, we are missing out on what we are called to do as followers of Christ. In fact, the rituals are there to help us become "good fruit" they are not an end in themselves. So, the next time you pick up a piece of fruit, ask yourself if you are doing all you can to live the life Jesus wants you to live. In a world that has plenty of bad bananas... be a good fruit!

(I think I'll just stick with bacon!)

Deacon Mike

Year A
Third Sunday of Advent
December 15, 2019

James 5:7-10/

I Want Patience Now!

A man observed a woman in the grocery store with a three-year-old girl in her cart. As they passed the cookie section, the child asked for cookies and her mother told her "no." The little girl immediately began to whine and fuss, and the mother said quietly, "Now Ellen, we just have half of the aisles left to go through; don't be upset. It won't be long." He passed the mother again in the candy aisle. Of course, the little girl began to shout for candy. When she was told she couldn't have any, she began to cry. The mother said, "There, there, Ellen, don't cry. Only two more aisles to go, and then we'll be checking out." The man again happened to be behind the pair at the check-out, where the little girl immediately began to clamor for gum and burst into a terrible tantrum upon discovering there would be no gum purchased today. The mother patiently said, "Ellen, we'll be through this checkout stand in five minutes, and then you can go home and have a nice nap." The man followed them out to the parking lot and stopped the woman to compliment her. "I couldn't help noticing how patient you were with little Ellen..." The mother broke in, "My little girl's name is Tammy... I'm Ellen."

Patience is a hard thing for many of us to master. In our second reading today from the book of James, the author talks about patience, not in everyday living but in our faith life. He knows that patience breeds endurance to overcome many of life's challenges. Many yearn for the peace that patience can bring and very few possess it. Being patient in our faith life is about letting others have the time to let God work in their life like he has worked in ours. One way to do that is to be attentive to the blessings we have in our life and finding ways of being a blessing in the life of others.

Rejoice! The coming of the Lord is at hand! Let him find us patiently waiting!

Deacon Mike

Year A
The Holy Family of Jesus, Mary, and Joseph
December 29, 2019

Colossians 3:12-21

5… 4… 3… 2… 1

We will soon be ushering in a new year. Many take this time to reflect on the past year to see if changes are needed. For some it might be financial changes, for others it might be physical changes (time to knock the dust off the treadmill), and for others there may be more substantial changes like adding a child to the family or changing jobs or career. Whether changes are great or small, the new year offers the opportunity to assess life.

One of the things that can get overlooked when we think about making changes is our spiritual life. I think most of us think about changes in our spiritual life as making more time for prayer or spending more time at church. While these are both really good items to add to the list of new year's resolutions, the reading from Paul to the Colossians today might give us more to think about.

He tells us to put on compassion, kindness, humility, gentleness, patience, and forgiveness.

If we are really looking to make a change in our life that can make a difference not only for ourselves but for the world, we may want to give some thought to Paul's words. It is great to want to improve ourselves because it shows an appreciation for the gift of life. If we try to be more compassionate, kind, humble, gentle, patient, and forgiving, we praise our Creator with gifts beyond measure.

Happy New Year!

Deacon Mike

Year A
The Epiphany of the Lord
January 5, 2020

Epiphany

Be the Star!

Have you ever thought about what it might be like to have lived in a different time? When things get busy and I can't get a moment's peace because technology follows me wherever I go, I wonder what it would have been like to live in a time before electricity was available? There is no doubt that life would have been much more physically demanding, but I can't help but think that it was easier to find an inner peace. No phones, no computers, no television, no way of really knowing the world's problems.

The reality, however, is that I live here and now. If I believe in a Creator, then I believe that I have been chosen for this place and time for a reason; not just me, but all of us! To think of the millions of events that had to happen to bring all of us here together now is mind-boggling. But if we think of a Creator that has said, "I have chosen you to be here now for a purpose," then we should try and find out what that purpose is supposed to be.

Today we celebrate the Epiphany of the Lord. We hear that familiar story of the magi following a start to find the newborn king of the Jews. This story should nudge us to ponder why Jesus was chosen to live in that place and time. (In fancy theological terms this is called the scandal of particularity.) It's fine that Jesus lived when he did, but I think the world could really use Jesus here and now!

The truth is Jesus is here and now and is alive in the hearts of all who believe! It is up to us to spread the Good News in our own time and place. We have been chosen to be in this place at this time. The world needs Jesus… the world needs you! The magi had a start to guide them to Jesus. Be the star that helps others find Jesus!

Deacon Mike

Year A
The Baptism of the Lord
January 2, 2020

Matthew 3:13-17

I really like a good "who-done-it?" I especially like it when the writer is clever enough to keep the suspense going right up until the end. When it is done extremely well, it seems like some of the character's roles are reversed and you end up saying, "I didn't see that coming!" Whether in a book or a movie, the element of surprise makes it worth reading or watching.

In our gospel today, we have that kind of surprise as Jesus approaches John the Baptist. If we didn't already know the outcome, we would say that Jesus was going into the desert to baptize John as he gets ready to begin his public ministry, and by the account in the gospel, John was expecting that too! But Jesus had other ideas.

Jesus needed to fulfill the plans of his Father and so he had to be baptized by John, not so that he would be holy, but so that the water would become holy! All who are baptized are baptized in those same, holy, waters. It is a twist that many did not see coming!

The Bible is full of stories that have surprise endings. The weak overcome the strong many times and those that do not speak well (think Moses) lead entire nations from captivity. So when God touches your heart to do something that may seem out of place, do not be so quick to dismiss it. God could be writing a surprise into your story!

Deacon Mike… (or is it?!)

Year A
Second Sunday in Ordinary Time
January 19, 2020

Isaiah 49:3, 5-6

Just One More Sit Up!

Lose weight, improve your posture, regrow your hair, workout more… the beginning of the year brings the onslaught of advertising aimed at those who made a new year's resolution to change some aspect of their life, usually involving appearances. Advertisers know how much of an emphasis the world places on looks and they are not shy about trying to make others feel like they are deficient in some way. The first reading today, however, tells us how God see us as Isaiah says, "I am made glorious in the sight of the LORD!"

God does not see us how others see us, (or even how we see ourselves sometimes). God does not see our flaws (either inner or outer) but instead sees the potential that is locked inside waiting to come out. Each of us is formed in the womb by God to be his child and he patiently waits as he allows us to come to understand that as his child, we are made in his image and likeness.

As we begin to see ourselves as children of God, we start to see the beauty within ourselves and then we begin to see the beauty in others. As God says to Isaiah, "I will make you a light to the nations!" So, the next time you look in the mirror and begin to notice a flaw, just remember that if it is God that is looking back, all he sees is his beautiful child. See yourself as God sees you and be a light to others!

Deacon Mike

Year A
Third Sunday in Ordinary Time
January 27, 2020

1 Corinthians 1:10-13, 17

Don't Forget the Packing Tape

I belong to Paul, I belong to Apollos, I belong to Cephas, "Chloe's people". It seems like the people of Corinth were going through an identity crisis! But I can't help but compare our current culture with that small city in the Mediterranean some two thousand years ago. We, like the Corinthians, tend to assign ourselves to certain groups and most of us certainly find it easy to assign others to certain groups! The problem is that we assign others to groups because it makes it easier for us to keep them labeled rather than find out who they really are. This is Paul's frustration in the second reading today.

When we label others, we are really putting them into a box and everything we come to know about that person needs to fit into that box. Once we have all of these boxes then we start to place similar boxes into bigger boxes and eventually those boxes go into bigger boxes. It is kind of how the brain works so it can retrieve information later. The problem is that we can end up with relatively few boxes and over time it becomes easy to just put people into one of our big boxes. It is a convenient way of not needing to get to know them.

One of the great benefits of my ministry is having the opportunity to really get to know others and to hear their stories. It has helped me to realize that people are complex beings that can fit in many boxes. Even if they place themselves in a specific box, as followers of Christ we can help everyone realize they are so much more than just belonging to this group or that group. I have come to know some really wonderful people just by listening to their story with some surprises along the way. So take some time to really get to know someone before placing them in their box… who knows, they may go into a completely different box than what you expected!

Deacon Mike

Year A
The Presentation of the Lord
February 2, 2020

Hebrews 2:14-18

No more Homework, no more Books…

I am happy to report that my collegiate career is quickly coming
to an end! After my thesis review in mid-February the only thing
left to do is walk the aisle to receive my diploma in May. Even
though I like to read and write, after several years of studies it
will be nice to not have to worry about turning in assignments or
taking tests. Let's be honest, there are not many people who
enjoy being tested (other than those who know they will do well)!
So, it is no surprise that most people do not enjoy it when life
seems to be testing them on a regular basis.

Unfortunately, being tested seems to just be a part of life and it
can come in many forms. It may be certain people in our lives. It
may be our finances. It may be our health or the health of a
loved one. It may be an inability to seem to connect with our
family. The list could go on and it is different for everyone. But
what seems to be universal is that when you are in the midst of a
trial, it can seem like it will never end.

One thing that can help is to remember that God does not put us
to the test. Like any loving parent, however, he may allow trials
in our lives so that we can learn to grow. Through challenges, we
learn about our own capacity and we learn to strengthen areas of
our character that may be weak. Even though we do not like
being tested, it can lead us to be better versions of ourselves.

Finally, we need to remember that we are not alone in our trials.
In the letter to the Hebrews today, we are reminded that we have
a savior who was tested through his suffering and so is able to
help us when we are tested. So, when you feel tested beyond
your strength, call on Jesus to help you through… he's been
there too.

Has anyone seen my #2 pencil?

Deacon Mike

Year A
Fifth Sunday in Ordinary Time
February 9, 2020

Matthew 5:13-16

The Sun and the Son

Maybe it's just me, but it seems like the sun has been a rare
commodity this winter. I can generally tolerate the cold (within
reason) but only if it is sunny. The sun brings a warmth that can
penetrate even the coldest of days. Without the sun, I find it
difficult to find something to warm me in the same way. Yes, I
can drink hot beverages or maybe take a warm shower, but it is
just not quite the same.

In our gospel today, Jesus gives us some images of what his
followers mean to the world. They (we) are the salt of the earth
and a light to the world. But those images come with some
cautions too. Once salt loses its taste, it really isn't good for
anything and a light does not do any good when it is hidden.
These images should be challenges for us.

What are we doing to make sure that we retain our "flavor" for
Jesus? Do we rely on just coming to Mass or do we seek other
avenues to help keep our faith strong? And what about our light?
Do we let it shine for others or do we tend to hide our light for
fear of being seen by others as a Christian?

The world needs us. Those that do not see the light coming from
us will try to find some other light. We are like the sun on a
winter's day. We can radiate the warmth and light of Christ to
those who are shivering in the darkness of their lives and really
make a difference to those in need. Do not be afraid to let your
light shine brightly to others! It may be exactly what they need to
keep them warm!

Deacon Mike

Year A
Sixth Sunday in Ordinary Time
February 16, 2020

Matthew 5:17-37

Uh… Well… Maybe…

Most of us learn at an early age that there are consequences for our actions. All you need to do is listen to a three-year-old spin a tale of how something became broken to realize that as quickly as we learn there are consequences, we try and find ways of defending our actions. I think that (over time) most Christians learn that trying to defend actions we know are wrong goes against the gospel message.

At the end of today's gospel, Jesus sums it up this way, "Let your 'yes' mean 'yes', and your 'no' mean 'no'." It is his way of telling his followers that the covenant (think Ten Commandments) handed to the Israelites is not compromised by his coming but is being brought to its fullness. What this says to us is that we know what is right and what is wrong and any attempt on our part to circumvent what is righteous does not come from God. This often takes the form of the "yeah-buts."

This is what we say when we do or say something we know is not totally true or just. When I was younger, it usually involved those I hung out with… "yeah-but my friends were doing it!" As we mature, life becomes more complex and arguments become more nuanced. For most of us the yeah-buts still hang around and the consequences became more serious. Trust is compromised, integrity is surrendered, and hearts are broken. What we say and do matters.

Yes or No?

Deacon Mike

Year A
Seventh Sunday in Ordinary Time
February 23, 2020

Leviticus 19:1-2, 17-18 / Matthew 5:38-48

This is a Public Service Reminder…

Lent begins on Wednesday.

Let's get the "mechanics" of Lent out of the way first. Ash
Wednesday and Good Friday are days set aside for fasting. The
guidelines for fasting will be in various publications so I will not
go into the details here. The remaining Fridays in Lent are days
of abstinence. Traditionally, Catholics abstain from eating (flesh)
meat on Fridays during Lent to honor Christ who gave up his
flesh on a Friday. The entire season of Lent focuses on the three
aspects of prayer, fasting, and almsgiving (charity).

Our readings today give us even more to think about during Lent.
From the reading in Leviticus: "You shall love your neighbor as
yourself." From the reading in Matthew: "But I say to you, love
your enemies and pray for those who persecute you."

Sometimes I think it is easier to just "do" the sacrifices and gloss
over the real challenge to love those around us that are not easy
to love. But the readings today certainly point towards working
on our relationships with others as the task before us. In the end,
however, it is not a situation of either/or… it is a situation of
both/and. We can make our sacrifices and work on loving our
neighbor at the same time. In fact, our prayers and sacrifices can
be directed toward those we find the hardest to love.

And remember… The Lord is kind and merciful… we should be
too!

Deacon Mike

Year A
First Sunday of Lent
March 1, 2020

Psalm 51

Walk the Lenten Walk, Talk the Lenten Talk

In the Liturgy of the Hours, the first psalm in the morning prayer
on Fridays is Psalm 51; it happens to be our responsorial psalm
today. In the psalm, the writer says to God that they are a sinner.
They acknowledge that they have done things that are not
pleasing to God. Next, they turn to God to ask to be refreshed,
renewed, and to continue to receive God's grace. Finally, they
vow that if God grants them forgiveness, they will go forth to
praise God!

This psalm provides a wonderful example for our Lenten journey!
We should spend the first part of Lent to (genuinely) examine our
lives. Are there aspects of our life that may not be living up to the
gospel? Are there things that we should be doing that we are not
doing? After our examination, we turn to ask for healing through
God's grace. This is an important step because it allows us to
come humbly before God to ask for his favor and continued
presence in our life. Finally, when our Lenten journey is through,
we should not be afraid to praise God for the gifts given to us.

The Lenten season really is a great treasure of the Church. It
allows all of us to break out of the mechanical day-to-day living
and focus in on what is important in our life. The psalmist knows,
as we should too, that our God is great in mercy. There is
nothing that we could ever to do to take us out of the reach of
God's loving arms. This Lent do not be afraid to go a little deeper
and experience God's overwhelming love for you!

Deacon Mike

Year A
Second Sunday of Lent
March 8, 2020

2 Timothy 1:8-10

Polka Dot Sofa… Really?

I am sure that most of us are familiar with the home improvement shows on television where the homeowners give the hosts carte blanche to transform a room or an entire house as they see fit. While most of these shows have a good ending where the owners are amazed at the transformation, there are a few that say, "Well… that's nice" in a way that you can tell they are not thrilled. I don't know about you, but I would have a hard time letting someone else decorate or remodel our house because I would be too anxious about the outcome.

In our second reading today, the writer tells Timothy that, "God saved us and called us to a holy life, not according to our works but according to his own design…" This is a reminder that our "work" does not lead to salvation but is simply the fruit of God's design for our life. And just like giving a decorator full reign over a house, I think it can make us uneasy to think of giving God full reign to design our life.

What we need to remember is that God is the ultimate designer and will shape our lives to something far better than we could ever imagine! In your Lenten journey, why not give God some freedom to help design your life? The Creator of the cosmos wants to give you the best life possible through his loving grace. Can you give him the keys?

Where is my hot glue gun?

Deacon Mike

Year A
Third Sunday of Lent
March 15, 2020

Psalm 95

Stone is Hard, Our Hearts Shouldn't Be

Now that my classes are done, I have time to get reacquainted
with my workshop and all the projects that have been
accumulating over the past few years. It feels good to get the
dust knocked off equipment (literally) and to take raw pieces of
wood and form them into something beautiful and useful. What is
frustrating, however, is to open a container of putty, finish, or
glue and find that it is all hard and crusty after sitting so long.
This means stopping what I was doing to make a run to the store
to get a fresh supply in order to continue. Ugh.

Our responsorial psalm today is Psalm 95 and our refrain is, "If
today you hear his voice, harden not your hearts." The psalmist
is recalling the Israelites journey in the desert and when the
grumbled against God for leading them away from their captivity
in Egypt because their journey became tedious. They hardened
their hearts against God who called them "stiff-necked" because
of their rebellion… there were hard to work with because of their
obstinance.

When we have a hardness in our hearts… when we refuse to
forgive others or to be open to the love of God… we make it hard
for God to work with us too. We may not think it is a big deal, but
just like finding that container of hardened glue right when it is
needed, God feels the same way when he is ready to use us and
we are hardened in our heart and not able to be used. Lent is the
perfect time to examine our lives to see if we are ready for what
God has in store for us. Prayer, fasting, and tending to the needs
of the poor are great ways to make sure we are fresh and ready
to go!

Oh great, now I'm out of sandpaper!

Deacon Mike

Year A
Fourth Sunday of Lent
March 22, 2020

Start of the Covid-19 Pandemic

The Lord is My Shepherd, there is Nothing I Shall Want

As I write this column, it seems like the world is in full panic mode over the latest coronavirus (there have been others.) As I watch events unfold and as the situation changes, I am struck by the fear that has gripped so many people, and my heart aches. My heart aches because I see a world that lives as though they are in control of life and when something happens that is beyond their control… well… the result is what we are experiencing.

The words "do not be afraid," "fear not," or "trust in me" appear in scriptures over 300 times! More than any other phrase. This seems to be a message that our Creator wants us to understand, and more importantly, live by. God is love and one of the fruits of that love is peace. God wants all of us to live in His peace!

We are the light of the world and the salt of the earth. The world needs us to show what it is like to live in the peace of Christ. We do not minister to others out of fear… we do it through love. So, as we journey through these unique times, let us do what is necessary to keep ourselves and our families healthy, but let us do so with the hope that this virus will be contained and run its course so that the world can stop operating out of fear. Let us shine our light!

Where did my toilet paper go?

Deacon Mike

Year A
Fifth Sunday of Lent
March 29,2020

Romans 8:8-11

Putting on the Ritz

One of Lisa and my favorite films is Young Frankenstein. A Mel
Brooke's film with a star-filled cast in a movie that spoofs the
earlier, classic Frankenstein movies. Scene after scene seems to
have some sort of twist to the original films that makes you laugh
or chuckle. One scene in particular that is recited at our house
quite often is when Dr. Frankenstein (Gene Wilder) and Igor
(Marty Feldman) are in a cemetery digging up a recently
deceased body to use in their experiment. As they lift the coffin
from the grave, Dr. Frankenstein says, "What an awful job." Igor
says, in reply, "It could be worse, it could be raining." And
immediately the skies open up and a downpour begins.

When Lisa or I find ourselves complaining a little too much about
something, the other will chime in with, "It could be worse, it
could be raining." Not only does this usually lighten the mood,
but it is also a good reminder that almost always things could be
worse than they are at the moment.

There is no doubt that life is challenging for so many right now.
Even if we are not personally affected by the COVID-19 virus, we
likely know someone who's life is in turmoil because of it. Aside
from the virus itself, people are working from home, kids are not
in school, those in the medical field are being tested to their
limits, businesses are closed or are limited, and almost everyone
seems to be a little on edge about the unknown of what all of this
will bring. It is easy in these times to be focused on the negative.

In our second reading, Paul reminds the Romans that they live in
the Spirit of God, not in the flesh. This applies for us too. We
have been given a great gift through our baptism that the Holy
Spirit dwells in each of us. But with this gift comes the
responsibility that as we care for the physical needs of our
family, friends, and neighbors, we must also make sure they are
spiritually cared for as well. Let people know that you are praying
for them through whatever means are appropriate. Cards, letters,

phone calls, and emails are all great ways to spread the Good News that even though things may seem bleak in the world, God will take of his children.

"I have promised, and I will do it, says the LORD."

Now go wash your hands!

Deacon Mike

Year A
Palm Sunday
April 5, 2020

Matthew 26:14—27:66

Meeting Jesus on the Cross

With so much commotion going on in the world right now, time has slipped away. It is hard for me to believe that it is Palm Sunday weekend already! Even though we will not be able to come together as a community, I encourage everyone to take the time to participate in a televised or web-based Mass this weekend to be able to live out the reading of the Passion of Jesus. I don't know if there is a greater story that brings together Jesus' humanity and divinity. That can be a great comfort for us, but it can be a challenge as well.

We believe that God desired to be with us so completely that he lived through some of the most painful and heartbreaking experiences of humanity. Jesus was spit on, beat, humiliated, made to carry his deathbed, and had his body nailed to a piece of wood.

And yet, he conquered all of that and more.

We should find solace in the fact that Jesus experienced the bitterness of humanity so that when we reach out to him, we do so with the confidence that he knows. He knows what it is like to be shamed, hurt, sad, hungry, and abandoned by his closest friends. He knows what it is like to live through trials both big and small. Meeting Jesus on the cross in our times of struggle should bring us hope in dark times.

The challenge to us is when we are the ones that are comforted, included, and well-cared for, because we are still called to meet Jesus on the cross. Because he is bound and helpless on the cross, he relies on us to do his work of caring for the outcast, the poor, the shamed, the sick, and the anxious. Jesus needs you in both good times and in bad.

How will you meet Jesus on the cross today?
Deacon Mike

Year A
Second Sunday of Easter (Divine Mercy Sunday)
April 19, 2020

1 Peter 1:3-9

Eat Your Karats!

In the second reading today, the first letter of Peter talks about how wonderful it is that God gave us a new birth through the resurrection of Jesus. He says that this is cause for great rejoicing BUT we may have to suffer through various trials so that our faith can become more and more genuine. The author likens it to the process of purifying gold. In ancient times, a dangerous process.

The gold was put into a crucible (a container that could withstand intense heat) and place into a fire. Bellows pumped air into the fire so that it became super-hot with temperatures approaching 1000 degrees! As the gold liquified, impurities known as dross would rise to the top and the refiner would have to skim off the elements that were not gold. This process would be repeated until nothing was left but pure gold.

Many may feel like we are being refined like gold right now! It seems like every day some new trial is coming our way and it can feel like it will never end. It will. The question is what do we do with our trials even when there doesn't seem to be an end in sight? Do we worry and complain about circumstances that are beyond our control, or do we have the courage to look at ourselves to see if there is an aspect that could be improved?

Nobody likes to go through trials, but that is where growth is most likely to occur. Trials cause us to be stretched in ways that hurt, but when we survive them, we become more flexible and ready to handle the next challenge just a little better. If you want an example, just ask a parent who had to recently teach their children how to multiply fractions!

Keep smiling!
Deacon Mike

P.S. – Wash your hands!

Year A
Third Sunday of Easter
April 26, 2020

1 Peter 1:17-21

The Journey

I will have to admit I am longing for the day when our travel restrictions are lifted, and we are able to move about freely. With warm weather on the horizon the itch to get out and see some sights is only going to grow. It will be a great day when we can get in the car and go places and experience new things again. I had to postpone a trip to see my niece who recently moved to Florida due to the current situation, so I hope to get that rescheduled soon! Ah… to travel again!

In the second reading today, the author of 1 Peter uses a word similar to "travel" but maybe a little weightier. He uses the word "sojourning" to talk about our walk here on earth. It is a word that we should pay attention to because to sojourn means only to stay someplace temporarily. The impact of this word in terms of our faith is huge because it reminds us that our journey here on earth is not permanent… we are simply passing through.

To know that we are sojourners here on earth should allow us to have a prospective on life that others may not. We know that we will have times of great joy and also great sorrow. We know that sometimes life will be easy and other times it will be hard. No matter what, though, life is only a stop along the way. The resurrection of Jesus assures us that we have been ransomed from this life to a life beyond all imagination in his Kingdom.

So, what do we do with this knowledge? Do we live our lives as if any of this matters or do we just "go with the flow" of what is popular at the time? Do we put our faith in Jesus that he really did die for us and rise from the dead or does our faith lie somewhere else? How do we mark our sojourn here on earth?

I'm tired of Googling how to get to the kitchen!

Deacon Mike

Year A
Fourth Sunday of Easter
May 3, 2020

1 Peter 2:20b-25

Ready… Set… Wait!

A few years ago, one of the satellite providers had a series of commercials to promote their newest product. They played upon the unique Boston accent of a family in various settings. In one of the commercials three men from the family are watching a news broadcast on a tablet in the kitchen as the reporter announces that the most dangerous place to be in a house is in the kitchen. In a thick, Bostonian accent, the father says, "Wee gotta git outta heer." As the commercial progresses, every place they go has a similar outcome always followed by, "Wee gotta git outta heer." Lisa and I use this phrase often, especially if one of us is running a bit behind to go to a meeting!

I am sure I am not alone in waiting for the day when the current "safer-at-home" orders are lifted, and we can move about more freely. Do not get me wrong, I love being at home and found time to slow down, find some peace, spend more time with Lisa, and get some projects done that have been on the back burner. But losing the freedom to move about is testing my patience.

In the second reading today from 1 Peter, the author says that, "If you are patient when you suffer for doing what is good, this is a grace before God." This is an excellent reminder for me that it is a great gift to learn to be patient especially when things are not going well. All trials in life eventually pass but it how we react to our trials that matter. No matter when trial you may be experiencing in your life, pray for help to endure it with patience and grace. Call upon Jesus who knows what it is like to suffer and to claim the victory! By his wounds you have been healed!

Deacon Mike

Year A
Fifth Sunday of Easter
May 10, 2020

1 Peter 2:4-9

What is Your Cornerstone?

In the area where I work, there has been an increase in the number of new buildings and houses that have been built in the last few years. It is interesting for me to drive past constructions sights on a regular basis to see how the building progresses. For most projects, it seems like it takes a lot of time to get the foundation and the framework completed, but once that is done, the exterior goes on quickly. I think it shows that if there is a well-planned, solid foundation and framework; the rest of the building process goes much more smoothly.

In the second reading today from 1 Peter, the author uses the analogy of building to describe our spiritual journey. Drawing upon the building techniques of the day, he highlights the most important stone of any building… the cornerstone. Without modern tools and techniques of laser levels and gps, the cornerstones in ancient buildings were used to set the course for the rest of the building. It had to be square, level, and solid unlike the cornerstones of most modern buildings that are decorative and have information about the date of construction and the builder.

The letter goes onto say that Jesus Christ needs to be the cornerstone of our spiritual lives. If we start to build on anything else, we are likely to have trouble. If we choose to use things of the world to be our cornerstone, then we become like them… mostly decorative without much use or substance. But if we begin with Jesus as our cornerstone, we come to live our calling as "a royal priesthood" and "we are precious in the sight of God."

Has anyone seen my trowel?

Deacon Mike

Year A
Sixth Sunday of Easter
May 17, 2020

1 Peter 3:15-18

Please Let it be Multiple Choice!

I am sure that most of us can recall a time in school when we were not prepared for a quiz, test, or exam. As the papers were being passed out, anxiety levels increase, fingers and palms become moist, and a million things are running through the mind. It is not a pleasant feeling, so the best course of action is to not be caught unprepared. By keeping up with the topic at hand, the anxiety and panic can be put aside and the task at hand can be done without the burden of an overwhelmed mind.

In the second reading today, the author of 1 Peter tells us, "Always be ready to give an explanation to anyone who asks you for a reason for your hope…" Even though this statement is in one of the epistles (letters in the New Testament), it is at the core of being on mission for Jesus. We need to always be ready to share our faith with others! But unlike a test in school, if we are not prepared to share what Jesus has done for us, we are not the ones who fail, it is the other person who fails because they do not receive the message of Jesus.

There are many who think that it is the job of the clergy to help others encounter Jesus. I think a better statement is that it is the Church's responsibility to help others encounter Jesus, because the Church is everyone who has been baptized. Every person in the Church is called to help bring others to Jesus and the best way to do that is to be ready to share what Jesus has done for you. Unlike a quiz, there is no single right or wrong answer because we are each touched by Holy Spirit in different ways. By sharing what Jesus means to you, there is only a right answer and you help to spread the Kingdom of God here on earth. So, take some time to reflect what Jesus means to you and be ready to share your story with others.

We should be ready to share our story with others:

A.   When it is convenient
B.   When I am in a good mood
C.   When I am with friends
D.   Always

Good luck!

Deacon Mike

Year A
The Ascension of the Lord
May 24, 2020

Matthew 28:16-20

Family Ties

It is hard to believe in this day and age, but I actually grew up knowing all of my grandparents and four of my great grandparents! Not just them being alive, but actually knowing them! It was only a few years ago that my last remaining grandparent passed away… my mom's mom. As the oldest grandchild I was asked to read her obituary at her funeral. I did really well until I got to the part that talked about her love of flowers. Instantly, a flood of memories came to mind and I got so emotional that it took me a couple of minutes to recover. I think some of it was the realization that I had to say goodbye not only to my grandma, but to an entire generation of my family. I have such great memories of my grandma even now I still smell the tea brewing and the jar of homemade oatmeal cookies being opened. Good days and simpler times.

Today, we celebrate the feast of the Ascension. The time when Jesus is taken up to heaven and his followers are instructed that they are the ones who have to carry out his message and his mission. Even though Jesus is able to explain his departure in more detail than the first time, I am sure that some of the disciples were still not ready to see Jesus ascend to his father. Not just for the fact that they would not see him again, but also coming to the realization that they would be on their own and were the ones who would be in charge of the mission.

I think that there may be many of us who may be feeling that way about the times we are living now. We used to go about our lives taking so many things for granted like going to the store, going out to eat at a restaurant, or most importantly, coming to mass. We have had to come to the realization that the church is not just the physical building where we meet, but that the church is us. Maybe more specifically, the church is you! And although we may not really want to take on that responsibility (just like the disciples) we have Jesus' promise to us just as he promised them; I am with you always, until the end of the age. I pray that when we are able to come back together as a church family that we find that many of our members have "grown up" and are ready to take their rightful place in the church. Some speculate that this pandemic will change our lives forever… maybe so… time will tell. But if we rise to the occasion the world will never be in lack of the love of Jesus regardless of what happens in the coming months and years!

Can I move up from the kid's table now?

Deacon Mike

Year A
The Most Holy Trinity
June 7, 2020

2 Corinthians 13:11-13

What About Social Distancing?!

Ask just about any boy or man and they can tell you about one of life's great embarrassments... being kissed by relatives when you are an adolescent. The sad part is that you can see it coming and there's nothing you can do about it. The best you can hope for is to escape while your well-meaning aunt talks to your parents! But really, that only postpones the inevitable. While being smooched on the cheek by lesser-known relative may be embarrassing, they are only doing what comes naturally, and today's second reading reinforces the practice.

In Paul's letter the Corinthians, he exhorts them to live peacefully together, to encourage one another, and to greet each other with a holy kiss. This is all fine and good, but what if someone approaches you that you don't get along with, or they have done or said something to harm you? Paul seems to be saying that the important thing is to find a way to make up with your sister or brother so that you can live in peace. It is one thing to be able to tolerate someone you don't care for; it is entirely different to be able to greet them with a kiss or some other intimate gesture like an embrace.

In order to slow down the current coronavirus, we have lost the ability to greet others with any kind of intimacy at all, but this cannot deter us from finding ways of engaging with others... even those we may not get along with. Being socially isolated makes it easy to forget about the "other" and focus only on ourselves, but we are called to find creative ways of staying engaged. Making a phone call, typing out an email, or writing a quick note are all ways to help keep our skills sharp so that we do not lose our focus on the other. Our current situation will end at some point, let us make sure we are ready for that time.

OXOX

Deacon Mike

Year A
The Most Holy Body and Blood of Christ (Corpus Christi)
June 14, 2020

Deuteronomy 8:2-3, 14b-16a

Desert Journeys

The first reading today recalls the sojourn of the Israelites in their desert journey out of the land of Egypt. My first real desert journey was about seven years ago as we drove from Phoenix to the Grand Canyon. I have travelled quite a bit, but the desert landscape always seems kind of surreal to me. Just as there is field after field of soybeans, corn, and wheat here, there are just miles and miles of rocks in the desert. To think of travelling on foot through the desert for any length of time seems impossible to me. My heart goes out to those that had to travel through the desert with Moses for many, many years. I would probably be right there with the rest of the travelers in complaining about… well… everything!

While certainly not lasting forty years, we are currently making our way through our own desert, and just like a real desert, it is hard to find signs of life. Birthday, anniversary, wedding, and graduation celebrations have been put on hold. Those who are vulnerable are only able to see their families through a computer screen. The eyes of people who pass each other in the street or in the stores seem to say "enemy". Add to that the recent racial tensions gripping our country and it can seem like the world is falling apart. We are definitely travelling in the desert. Since travelling in the desert is harsh and the landscape unending, it can seem like the journey will never end… it will. The place to start is found in our reading,

"Do not forget the LORD, your God…"

If we keep our eyes fixed on the Lord, then no matter where our journey leads us, we will not give in to despair.

Peace be with you all,

Deacon Mike

Year A
Twelfth Sunday in Ordinary Time
June 21, 2020

Mathew 10:26-33

Truth Versus Fear

When I was a child, I was scared of thunderstorms. I think that
much of the reason came from the collective uneasiness of the
community because of what happened on Palm Sunday in 1965.
I have mentioned before that on that fateful day, 47 tornadoes
broke out over a three-state area. The county where we lived
was particularly hard hit. It was almost impossible to not have
known someone directly impacted by the storms that day. So, it
is understandable that many people became uneasy every time
a storm passed through the area. It took many years for me to
shake off being afraid of storms. It boiled down to trusting in my
own experience of living through many storms and coming
through unscathed rather than living in someone else's fear.

Fear is real and other than (literal) life or death situations, fear
becomes an impediment to living in truth and love. Today's
gospel is not overly lengthy, and yet Jesus tells his followers
three times to not be fearful of the things of this world. Jesus
knows that fear is in the woven into the fabric of who we are as
human beings, and so it takes an effort to keep that fear in
check. That is why knowing Jesus and drawing closer to him is
so important. One of the ways that we draw close to Jesus is
when we let our hearts search for what is true. This is not easy
because it requires us to examine what we believe and why.
There are not many who have the courage to do so.

But courage is exactly what Jesus is calling us to in our reading
today. Not courage in ourselves, but courage that come through
knowing that we are children of a loving Father. When things
seem to be spiraling out of control, it is easy to let our gaze shift
from God to things of this world, but Jesus is here to remind us
that, "all the hairs of your head are counted" and God prizes you
as one of his dearest children. Let us go forth confidently
knowing that if we are sincere in our search for the truth that
comes from God, we need not live in fear.
Deacon Mike

Year A
Fourteenth Sunday in Ordinary Time
July 5, 2020

Romans 8:9, 11-13

$12x + 4y = 120$ Solve for y

When I was in school, math was my favorite subject. Geometry, trigonometry, algebra, calculus… all of it. One of the reasons that I took to math is that it was logical to me. Follow the correct steps, pay attention to detail, and the correct answer followed. One of the things that I learned early on is that to do math well, it is critical to start out correctly. If the equation was not written out exactly right, there was no way to get the right answer. Having the correct equation did not guarantee a correct answer but starting off with an incorrect equation was fatal.

In the second reading today, Paul reminds the Romans that whoever does not have the Spirit of Christ does not belong to him. It is one of those statements that is easily glossed over as just another one of Paul's teachings, but if we dwell on it for a bit, there might be profound meaning for us today as well.

It is obvious to say that there is much tension in our world today. Politics, coronavirus, and racial divide are just the ones at the top of the list. The results of these tensions have been rather ugly, both physically and within relationships. This should be a stark reminder to us that spiritual darkness is real and that we have to be on guard at all times. We have to remember that we should not be feuding and fighting with each other, but against the darkness that is trying to divide us! We need to cling to the fact that through our baptism we have the Spirit of Christ in us to overcome the darkness of the world and that we should do everything we can to nurture that Spirit. It has to be core of where we start. If we don't begin with the Spirit of Christ, we have little chance of finding the correct solution. Find common ground. Find ways to unite. Find peace.

Deacon Mike

$y = 30 - 3x$

Year A
Fifteenth Sunday in Ordinary Time
July 12, 2020

Isaiah 55:10-11

Whether the Weather Will be Warm or Wrainy?

Most of you know that my parents live in Indiana, so we only get
to spend time with them every few months. Since that is the
case, I give them a call a couple of times a week just to check in
to see how things are going. It is inevitable that the conversation
at some point will turn to the weather (retired people love to talk
about the weather!) We swap reports about what the weather
has been like and how the lawn and gardens are faring. At this
time of the year, especially with the hot weather, it is common to
hear, "We could use some rain!" My parents have both flower
gardens and a vegetable garden, so getting rain is important for
them to flourish.

In the first reading today from Isaiah, we are reminded that the
word of God comes to us like rain or snow. This provides a visual
image that we can relate to because we can see the effects of
rain on the earth. When the ground is baked hard from the
summer sun and a storm produces a downpour of rain, it does
little good because most of the rain just runs off to find the lowest
spot. In order for rain to be beneficial, the ground needs to be in
a condition that is ready to receive the moisture. The same can
be said for us receiving the word of God.

If we are hardened, cynical, or bitter, the word of God will have a
hard time providing a benefit for us. Much like the hardened
ground, the message will simply bounce off of us and run away.
But if our hearts are cultivated in the ways of God, the Word will
provide abundant nourishment to help us grow and then we can
help others to grow. I think it is easy in our current time of strife
and uncertainty to become hardened to others and to God. If this
is the case, detach and find some peace and some time with
God. Be ready to receive God's word!

Looks like another hot one!
Deacon Mike

Year A
Sixteenth Sunday in Ordinary Time
July 19, 2020

Romans 8:26-27

Praying as We Ought

There are many examples in scriptures about people trying to
figure out what God's plan is for their life. It should really not
come as a surprise that once we acknowledge that God is real
that we want to try and figure out what God wants for us. This
even transcends into the secular world. In the early 90's there
was an obscure comedian by the name of Emo Philips. He did a
bit about how he believed in the power of prayer and that when
he was a little boy, he prayed every day for a new bicycle. After
praying for many days without any result, he realized that God
didn't work that way, so instead he stole a bike and asked for
forgiveness!

 All kidding aside, there are times when our prayer life could use
some help. Most people experience a "dryness" in their prayer
life every wondering if God is even listening. Once this dryness
sets in, it becomes increasingly harder to know how to pray and
that can lead to abandoning prayer altogether. What can we do
when we find ourselves wandering around in the forest of
prayer? The second reading today provides us with some
guidance when we feel lost or abandoned.

Brothers and sisters: The Spirit comes to the aid of our
weakness;
for we do not know how to pray as we ought, but the Spirit
himself intercedes with inexpressible groanings. And the one
who searches hearts knows what is the intention of the Spirit,
because he intercedes for the holy ones according to God's will.

In God's grand design, the Holy Spirit is available to us no matter
where we are at in our prayer life. If we find ourselves stuck in
prayer or not even knowing how to pray at all, we can simply call
on the Holy Spirit to intercede for us. I know that this has
become an important piece in my prayer life and every day I
conclude my prayers by asking the Holy Spirit to pray for me for
the things that are beyond my knowing. I rest knowing that the

Holy Spirit works all things for the glory of God! So if you find yourself needing a jump start to your prayer life… call on the Holy Spirit and see what a difference it can make in your life!

Deacon Mike

P.S. Please don't steal a bike.

Year A
Seventeenth Sunday in Ordinary Time
July 26, 2020

1 Kings 3:5, 7-12

The Humbleness of Wisdom

The 1960's show Gomer Pyle comes on in the evening about the time when Lisa and I are winding down our day. We are not huge fans of the show, but we will catch an episode every once in a while. One of the main characters that plays opposite of Gomer is his platoon sergeant. Through most episodes, Sergeant Carter spends his time yelling at Gomer about one thing or another simply because he is the sergeant, and it is his job to instill disciple and knowledge into his recruits. But time after time, Sergeant Carter misses out on what is really happening because he is so busy yelling his knowledge to others. Because of that, he creates a bigger mess that wastes much time and energy to clean up that could be used for a better purpose.

 Right now, it seems like much of the world is Sergeant Carter. There are many out there simply yelling their truth to others. Maybe not physically (although there is plenty of that too) but certainly online and in the media. But as the old adage goes, "If you are speaking, you are not listening." What is being missed by those that are so entrenched in their viewpoints? Most likely not anything that would change their core beliefs, but certainly they miss out on the nuances that other voices can bring to the table. Listening for understanding takes a humbleness to say, "Maybe I don't know it all."

In the first reading today, Solomon asks God for an understanding heart. God grants him his request not because it is the best thing that Solomon could have asked for, but because Solomon asked for it instead of a long life, riches, or dominance. God gives Solomon wisdom and understanding because Solomon humbled himself before God. I think there is a lesson for us in this passage that if we want to make a change in this world, our first step should be to humbly approach our savior and ask for wisdom and understanding. Be ready, however, for that wisdom and understanding to come from the person across from us!

Year A
Eighteenth Sunday in Ordinary Time
August 2, 2020

Romans 8:35, 37-39

Nested in the Love of God

For the past four months at work we have been: entertained, flummoxed, agitated, mesmerized, and baffled by a pair of mourning doves that continue to try and build their nest by the windshield wipers on the hood of cars in the parking lot. Despite the fact that every afternoon as people go home their days' work gets scattered by the roadside, this pair starts the next day by selecting their vehicle of choice to begin again. It is almost tragic to see their efforts be in vain, but it is also amazing to see their commitment to each other with the start of each new day.

Paul's letter to the Romans today lists seventeen obstacles that could separate his audience from the love of Christ. There are probably more that could be added to the list, and each generation could add their own struggles as well. Certainly, our own struggles with the current coronavirus have tested the faith of many. What Paul is talking about, however, isn't our love for Christ, but the love of Christ for us.

Just like those mourning doves start each day by trying to build their nest, Jesus starts each day by trying to build a relationship with every one of us. Even though we may choose to get in our "spiritual car" and drive away, Jesus is there every morning ready to build. How tenacious are we with our relationships? Yes, with Jesus, but what about our relationships with others? Paul believes that there isn't anything that can keep us from the love of Jesus. Are we able to start anew to build relationships that have been challenged by different obstacles? Paul believes that love conquers all… do we believe the same?

What's that cooing sound?

Deacon Mike

Year A
Nineteenth Sunday in Ordinary Time
August 9, 2020

1 Kings 19:9a, 11-13a

Speak a Little Louder Please!

I cannot pinpoint the exact time that I went from cranking up rock music in the car to turning down the volume on the radio when I am looking for a new street address, but there is no denying that it has happened! I am pretty sure the more "mature" readers of this article can identify with me! But really… what is up with that?! Why would loud music interfere with my ability to see? The answer is that loud music does not interfere with someone's ability to see, but it does affect the ability to concentrate. As it turns out, there is something called "attentional capacity" and it decreases as we get older. So, in reality, turning down the music really does help us our concentration and "see" better!

The reading today from 1 Kings is one of my favorites. Elijah is hiding from the Israelites who are looking to kill him, but God finds him and asks him why he is hiding. After explaining that he is being hunted, God wants to assure Elijah that he is with him, so he starts crushing rocks with wind and earthquakes, but Elijah does not find God in the chaos and the noise. It is a tiny, whispering sound that sends Elijah running to the cave entrance for fear of seeing God and dying.

There is not any lack of noise and chaos in our world today. There are very few who can escape the cacophony that only seems to get worse with every passing day. As the reading from 1 Kings points out, God is not found in the noise and the chaos, but in silence. In order to find God, we will need to find a way to find quiet and peace in our minds and hearts. Do not think that "attentional capacity" is just limited to the external senses, our internal senses are equally affected.

So, this week, try and find ways of living in the silence. When you find your silence, help others to find theirs. Together we can help each other turn down the noise of life to hear those tiny, whispering sounds that come from our Creator.
Party on Wayne… Party on Garth!

Year A
Twentieth Sunday in Ordinary Time
August 16, 2020

Romans 11:13-15, 29-32

Where is Theodor Geisel When You Need Him?

Dr. Suess books were a staple in my childhood library. Cat in the Hat, Green Eggs and Ham, Go, Dog, Go! and so many more! But more than just being whimsical children books, some of the stories conveyed great lessons. The story that keeps coming to my mind lately is the The Sneetches. The core of the story is that there were star-bellied Sneetches and Sneetches that did not have stars on their bellies. The star-bellied Sneetches thought they were above the plain-bellied Sneetches and treated them as inferior at every opportunity.

Enter Sylvester McMonkey McBean who had a machine that would put stars on the bellies that didn't have one for a sum of $3. All of the plain-bellied Sneetches went through the machine so that all the Sneetches had stars on their bellies. Conveniently, Mr. McMonkey McBean had a machine to remove stars from the bellies of the original star-bellied Sneetches for $10. As the story unfolds, all of the Sneetches keep going through both machines until they run out of money. The result is that no one could tell who was an original star-bellied Sneetch and who wasn't and they learned that in the end, it didn't matter at all. The link to the YouTube video of the story is https://www.youtube.com/watch?v=PdLPe7XjdKc if you have ten minutes free, I encourage you to watch.

There are two reasons this comes to mind today. The second reading from Paul to the Romans talks about how in the eyes of God, there is no difference between Jews and Gentiles, we are all in need of God's mercy. The other thing that comes to mind is our current circumstances and the conversations around facemasks. From we must wear one or everyone is going to die, to the virus is a hoax and everything in between, there are few people that have not formulated their own thoughts on the subject. Believe it or not, there are actually people that change their minds as new information becomes available! No matter where you are at on the continuum, please do not forget in the

end, we are all human beings in need of God's grace. In the end,
that is what is important.

Time to go to the marshmallow roast!

Deacon Mike

Year A
Twenty-first Sunday in Ordinary Time
August 23, 2020

Psalm 138:1-2, 2-3, 6, 8

Creative Process

Something that I have been working on is to find goodness in the midst of the effects of the current coronavirus. One of the ways that I have found goodness is in the creativity that has bloomed as people try to find ways of occupying their time at home. I really enjoy seeing the pride of those that have taken up woodworking, photography, painting, sewing, landscaping, home improvements and the like. Sometimes, the talent that has been displayed is nothing short of amazing! We are born to create because we are made in the image and likeness of a Creator God and when we create, we feel a connection with God.

Unlike God, many of our creations are less than perfect. Aside from a gifted few, it takes time and several attempts to hone a talent and those attempts usually do not make it onto Facebook or Twitter. They find their way to a remote corner of the house or perhaps get moved to the "do over" project list. I know my scrap bin of wood contains several specimens from projects gone awry. It is just part of the process in the creative cycle.

The responsorial psalm today says, "Do not forsake the work of your hands." It seems like the psalmist had some experience in having a creation go astray and calls out to God to not give up on his creations even though they may not be turning out how they were envisioned. Just like developing a talent takes time, patience, and the willingness to start over, some of those that we encounter are in that development stage. Instead of thinking that others are beyond hope, try to think of them as a work in progress and that we need to give the Creator time to work his masterpiece. Be kind. Be peaceful. Pray on!

Is it measure once and cut twice or measure twice and cut once?

Deacon Mike

Year A
Twenty-second Sunday in Ordinary Time
August 30, 2020

Psalm 63:2, 3-4, 5-6, 8-9

Reign Down

As I write this article, the area has not had much, if any, rain for about three weeks and it is beginning to show. Grass that was nice and green is going dormant to protect its roots. The day lilies around our house are deflating like a balloon with a slow leak and the pond and the bird baths are waiting room only! Even the ground itself is forming wide cracks and the clay soil begins to contract from the lack of moisture. Nature has a way of making it clear when it lacks the life-giving water that it needs.

The responsorial psalm today is one that is recited in the Liturgy of the Hours quite often. The opening paragraph has Isaiah saying, "for you my soul thirsts, in a land parched, lifeless, and without water." It is a stunning visual characterization of comparing a soul longing for God with land that is parched, lifeless, and without water. But I think there is a deeper meaning here too.

When the earth is dry, it lacks and craves only one thing… water. Cloud cover can help to lessen the effects by shading the scorching sun, but in the end, the only thing that will truly help is rain. When we experience times of dryness in our life, we can fill it with all kinds of things that will, like cloud cover, seem to lessen the effects of the dryness, but in the end, the only thing that will satisfy our longing is God.

There are many who are experiencing dryness in their life due to isolation brought on by the measures taken to slow the spread of the current coronavirus. Some of those will try to substitute many things for their true longing for God. Our parish has the opportunity to help everyone reconnect with God and with others through our Reconnect to Inspire initiative. Please consider joining a group… if not for you… offer it up as a sacrifice for others.
Where is my watering can?
Deacon Mike

Year A
Twenty-third Sunday in Ordinary Time
September 6, 2020

Matthew 18:15-20

A Path for Justice

Ever watch a couple of eight-year-olds argue back and forth about something? It might go something like this, "Yah-huh", "Uhn-uhn", "Yah-huh", "Uhn-uhn" (well, you get the picture.) At the center of the argument is something that each person claims to know as the truth and refuses to concede even if they are proven wrong! Holding on to being the one who is right outweighs any attempt at truth and justice.

The gospel today provides a different path for justice. If someone has done something to harm you, go and tell them alone. Many times, a direct and sincere approach can help solve what might otherwise be an ugly situation. Present what you know and why the other person hurt you and allow them the time to explain or apologize. If that doesn't work, then bring in someone who is trusted to listen to both sides and determine what is plausible. If that doesn't work, then more formal steps are necessary if the harm is grievous.

This sounds easy on paper but is hard to put into practice. Approaching someone that has harmed us does expose us to more harm, but we should also be a people that value truth and justice. We have the opportunity to show the world this path to justice that eliminates name-calling, half-truths, and hidden agendas. This is indeed an opportunity for Christians to practice what they preach!

I am rubber and you are glue… oh, never mind.

Deacon Mike

Year A
Twenty-fourth Sunday in Ordinary Time
September 13, 2020

Sirach 27:30—28:7 / Matthew 18:21-35

Being Set Up

Now that my schooling is done, I have been able to play more golf this summer. Over the past several years I have not been able to play much due to commitments, so it has been a joy to be back out on the course on a regular basis. That being said, I have struggled to get back to playing up to my ability. As with any sport, motor skills that were once almost automatic have fallen into the abyss (along with where did I put my phone, car keys, and glasses!) Anyway, what I have observed is that my struggles really centered around my lack of setting up properly before hitting a shot. Once I began taking the time to make sure my grip, my stance, and my posture were correct before trying the shot, my game improved dramatically. I think there is something here that can be tied into today's readings.

The readings for today are focused on what happens when we hold onto anger and vengeance. The reading from Sirach begins with, "Wrath and anger are hateful things, yet the sinner hugs them tight." The Gospel of Matthew relates the story of a servant that was forgiven their debt, and yet would not extend the same to those indebted to him. These readings point to the fact that we should be ready to forgive rather than to seek vengeance. In other words, we should work on our set up so that when we are confronted with things that trigger us, we do not act out harshly, but instead act like we expect others to act towards us.

There is much discord in our society. If the current coronavirus (and reactions to it) was not enough, we have racial unrest and an election to add fuel to the fire. There is much that can cause our anger and vengeance to grow. That is why it is important that we have the proper set up so that we can handle things with the love of our neighbor as our starting point. We should be set up to forgive rather than to hate. As the responsorial psalm says, "He pardons all your iniquities, and heals all your ills." We should be ready to do the same for others.
"Fore!" – There's that darn slice again!

Year A
Twenty-fifth Sunday in Ordinary Time
September 20, 2020

Philippians 1:20c-24, 27a

Be Vewy, Vewy Qwiet

One of the staples growing up in the 1960's was Saturday morning cartoons. The Jetson's, Mighty Mouse, Underdog, The Flintstone's, Tom & Jerry… the list could go on. The crown jewel of Saturday mornings, however, was Bugs Bunny and his cronies. I will have to admit that there are episodes that I could probably still recite almost word for word. One of the best animations features Bugs, Daffy Duck, and Elmer Fudd where they argue about it being duck season or rabbit season. There is a scene where Bugs and Daffy go back and forth, "It's duck season, it's rabbit season, it's duck season, it's rabbit season, it's rabbit season, it's duck season!" The clever Bugs Bunny outwits Daffy Duck by flipping the conversation to Daffy's detriment.

In the second reading today, Paul kind of sounds like the scenario above when he thinks about life and death in Jesus. "It's life, it's death, it's life, it's death"… Paul cannot decide if it would be better for him to live or to die. To live means that he can continue to do the work of an evangelist, to die means that he will live with Christ. In the end, he says that what is important is to live in a way that is worthy of the gospel of Christ.

When we choose empathy over anger, when we choose kindness over criticism, when we choose love over ideology… we choose to live to live in a way that is worthy of the gospel of Christ. It is then that just like Paul, Christ will be magnified through us. This is not beyond our reach, but simply lies in the choices that we make every day. Work to choose the next best thing in your life!

Now where is that wasscally wabbit?

Deacon Mike

Year A
Twenty-sixth Sunday in Ordinary Time
September 27, 2020

Ezekiel 18:25-28

She's Touching Me!

My sister is three years younger than me. For the most part we got along fine, but we both have a competitive streak and we both like to win (we are still banned by our mom from playing the card game "Dutch Blitz"). Anyway, this competitiveness would also play out in everyday circumstances. One of us would egg-on the other by touching, pinching, or some other annoying behavior and then wait for the retaliation. Of course, the one doing the retaliation would inevitably get caught by mom or dad and get scolded. This would be met with the response, "that's not fair, they did it first!" (We must have missed our calling to be elected officials)!

In the first reading today from Ezekiel, the Israelites are called to task by saying that the Lord's ways are not fair. The Lord, in turn, counters by asking if it is the Lord's ways that are unfair, or their ways that are unfair? But here's the twist… God takes it from a broad accusation and brings it to a personal level. It is up to the individual to choose what is right and just and to turn away from evil. There is something here that is useful.

As we journey through life, we can look to others to help shape society towards our beliefs and values. But when it comes right down to it, you and I are the ones who can affect change by examining our own lives, turning away from sin, and seeking the Lord's ways. We are knee deep in the election cycle, and it is easy to get caught up in thinking that if we vote this way or that way, we will get the outcomes we desire. Participating in the political process is our right and duty, but the readings today seem to suggest that if want real change for the world, we need to start by looking inward.

Seek the Lord's ways.

Deacon Mike

Year A
Twenty-seventh Sunday in Ordinary Time
October 4, 2020

Philippians 4:6-9

Think of These Things

Wow! Is it just me or did autumn seem to come out of nowhere this year? It seems like one day I was wearing shorts on the golf course and then the next day I was looking at all the leaves falling from the trees in the yard. I am not complaining though because fall is my favorite time of year. The beauty of fall colors, cool nights, and the endless activity of the critters in the yard are signs that nature is ready to begin winter's rest. I think most of us are ready for some rest of that chaos that 2020 has brought into our lives and maybe we can take a clue from nature and begin to quiet our hearts and minds so that the Holy Spirit can work on making us new again.

In Paul's letter to the Philippians today, he reminds them to meditate on the things that are true, honorable, just, pure, lovely, gracious, excellent, and worthy of praise. Paul seems to know that if we want true peace in our lives, that we need to focus on the things that are of God. This is not an easy thing to do because we seem to be bombarded with news on a daily basis that presents us with everything that seems to be contrary to what is listed above. But if we want peace in our lives, we need to draw towards the things that are from God and avoid the things that are not.

Paul tells the Philippians to keep doing the things they have learned and received. He is reminding them that they have been blessed to have a life in Christ. We need to remember the same.

Time to get Lisa's rake ready!

Deacon Mike

Year A
Twenty-eighth Sunday in Ordinary Time
October 11, 2020

Philippians 4:12-14, 19-20

Compound Interest

Paul's letter the Philippians in today's second reading always strikes a chord with me. My late teen years were in the seventies and early eighties. While interest rates today hover around zero, back then it was not uncommon to see interest rates on car loans at 15% with some above 20%! Times were really tough for my mom and I as each week was a test in budgeting skills. We did not have much at all. Having lived through that, I learned that having some savings to fall back on is a great thing and I have worked hard to stay as debt-free as possible and to save as much as I can. Like Paul, I have learned to live humbly and to live with abundance. But that's not the key.

At the end of today's passage, Paul notes of the kindness of the Philippians to share in his distress. While it is true that God can (and does) work in mysterious ways, I think that God mainly works through us and others. When we open ourselves to the workings of the Holy Spirit, then we can become the instruments that help to supply others with what they need. Physically, yes, but also spiritually and emotionally. In addition, when we are attuned to the Holy Spirit, we can be ready to receive through others.

I believe that God does supply us with all that we need. I also believe that much like saving money, we need to do whatever it takes to be in tune with the Holy Spirit so that we do not fall into spiritual poverty. Invest in your prayer life, invest in good friendships, invest in worship, and reap God's abundance!

Deacon Mike

Year A
Twenty-ninth Sunday in Ordinary Time
October 18, 2020

1 Thessalonians 1:1-5b

Being Chosen

The lessons learned on the elementary school playground at recess arguably outweigh what I learned in the classroom. Maybe not about academics, but certainly about life in general. Things like choosing your friends wisely and learning how news travels through the "grapevine" are lessons that still serve me well even today. One of the most important lessons that I learned on the playground is that life isn't always (what we think of as) fair. Some people are smarter than others, some are better looking, and some have more natural athletic talent.

The latter came to light when it was time to choose the teams for kickball or dodgeball. The two best athletes would become the captains and they would take turns choosing the best players from the ones remaining. This would inevitably lead to the final two kids to see who would get picked last, "okay I guess I'll take [insert name here]". Of course, this could be turned around when it was time to pick teams for the spelling bee, but somehow that didn't seem quite as important! When you were chosen in the process made a statement about where you fit in with the group and over time, everyone kind of got used to where they were chosen in the sequence. Every once in a while, there would be a surprise pick because of a recent performance, but for the most part, it went as expected and not all that important… most everyone got to play regardless.

In the letter to the Thessalonians, Paul reminds us that is important for us to know how we were chosen by God. We are not chosen because our intelligence, physical ability, or even our faithfulness. We are chosen with much conviction because we are loved by God. Not only that, but we are chosen with power through the Holy Spirit so that we can live out our faith to its absolute fullness! Being chosen by God means that we can excel far beyond anything we can imagine. Unlike being chosen for a sport, God wants everyone to be on his team because everyone brings something to the faith that others do not possess. You are chosen by God. You are needed by God.

No spinners!
Deacon Mike

Year A
Thirtieth Sunday in Ordinary Time
October 25, 2020

1 Thessalonians 1:5c-10

What Sort of People are We?

It was common practice as I was growing up to get "the talk" before going over to someone else's house. "Behave yourself, be nice, listen to what the grown up tells you, be polite, say 'please' and 'thank you,'" basically all of the things that we were taught on a regular basis. It was just a reminder that when we were in other people's homes to behave like we were supposed to behave. I grew up in a small town, so there were no secrets of who's children behaved well and who's children behaved poorly. "The talk" was meant to show others what kind of family we were.

In Paul's letter to the Thessalonians, he reminds them about what kind of person he was among them and that they, in turn, need to become a model for all believers. Paul knows that in order to bring Christ to others, the Thessalonians need to be model Christians. I think there is a case to be made that we (in general) have forgotten this truth. Poll after poll shows that self-identified Catholics tend to mirror the general public when it comes to subjects such as abortion, divorce, euthanasia, and belief in the presence of Christ in the Eucharist. For the most part, Catholics are indistinguishable from anyone else in the culture. But should we be that way?

Our national election is happening in a couple of days. We are being told by most media outlets to expect chaos to reign in the following days and weeks. Since the media make their money by selling fear and stoking division, I would tend to believe that things will sort themselves out just fine, it may just take a little longer than usual. In any event, we have the chance to show the world that, as followers of Christ, we have a different standard than to get caught up in the fray. We should act with kindness, patience, and to seek understanding no matter what political belief we hold dear. Our hope is in our Lord Jesus Christ, and that should tell others exactly what sort of people we are.
May God bless the USA!

Year A
Solemnity of All Saints
November 1, 2020

All Saints Day

How About Some Bacon Bits?

I know this may come as a shock to some of you, but I am not a big salad eater. By the time I put on enough toppings and dressing to make it interesting, the benefits of eating lettuce goes out the window. But every once and a while I will get a craving for a salad, and when I do, Lisa's reaction is, "Who are you, and what have you done with Mike?!" Not only is this way of getting in some good-natured ribbing, but it also shows a level of intimacy because only a person who knows me as well as Lisa could make that remark and have it be so accurate.

In the reading from 1 John today, the author tells us that God knows us so well that we are called his children. Not because of anything that we have done or haven't done, but simply because the Father has bestowed his love on us. Think about that. God knows us as intimately as parents know their children. Beyond our likes and dislikes, God knows how awesome we can be and knows when we fail to live up to our potential. Whether at our best, or at our worst, God still calls us his children.

Today we celebrate All Saints Day. The day when we commemorate those that have gone before us that commune with God in his Kingdom. This is the day when we are reminded that we are all called to heaven at the end of our earthly life. It is also a day that we are reminded that the path to Sainthood is rarely the same between two people. For some, their lives exemplified living a Christian life from the beginning, but for others it took some time for the Holy Spirit to break through. Just as any parent knows, every child develops different strengths and weaknesses, but their family would not be complete without them. God thinks of us in the same way…his family is not complete without you!

Where is that left-over Halloween candy?

Deacon Mike

Year A
Thirty-second Sunday in Ordinary Time
November 8, 2020

Laughter

The Wisdom of Laughter

I am fortunate to have grown up in a family that loved to laugh. Both sides of my family had a good sense of humor which led to many funny stories being told at family gatherings. One such (true) story is about my grandpa. He worked as a handyman for many years and was called upon to install the first stop and go light in the town where I was raised. Him and a couple of town workers spent the night installing the light so that it would be done by the next day. After installing the light, he got into his truck and waited for the light to turn red and then drove through the intersection. He told us that he did it because he wanted to be the first person to run the red light in town! There were also plentiful stories about my uncles on both sides of my family and their shenanigans.

It may just be me, but I sense that people are losing their ability to laugh. I get it. Life certainly has its challenges for most people right now and there doesn't seem to be much to laugh about. But laughter has some great benefits for us physically, mentally, and spiritually. Laughter can break tension, loosen muscles, and lift our spirits. Laughter does not diminish the circumstances of life but should provide a way to look at those circumstances to remind ourselves that no matter what we face, our circumstances do not have to define who we are! This is especially true of circumstances that are beyond our control.

Allow yourself to laugh.

Deacon Mike

A priest, a minister, and a rabbit walk into a bar, and the rabbit says, "I think I'm a typo!"

Year A
Thirty-third Sunday in Ordinary Time
November 15, 2020

Matthew 25:14-30

How Talented Are You?

I only have one sibling… my sister who is three years younger than me. Whenever it came to a decision about who would get the last of something (cookie, soda, candy, etc.) my mom would use the tried and true, "One of you divide it and the other gets to choose." It is amazing how quickly children can become geometry experts! I could cut a cookie with such precision it would me a surgeon jealous! All joking aside, it was a way that mom used to achieve a fair outcome.

I think that most of us would agree that a fair outcome is a good thing. That is why the gospel story today may get us rankled. Why is the servant punished who took great care to guard what was given to him that wasn't his? In fairness, it seems like this servant should at the very least be commended for not losing or spending the money that was given to him. Instead, the master chastises him for being lazy. If we focus on what we think is fair, this parable seems to be way out of character coming from Jesus. But if we only focus on what is fair, we may miss that this parable is really about what is demanded of us as children of the light.

To be clear, we are the servant who has been given the five talents. We are baptized Christians who have the love of God and belong to a community of believers who are there to help us on our way. We have been given more than what most of us will ever realize because it is in our nature to focus on what we don't have rather than what we do have. I am not talking about the physical here, but rather the spiritual. We have all been given certain spiritual talents and it is our responsibility to foster them and make them grow so that we can return them to God double what we were given. How do we do that? By sharing them with others so that they too can nurture their talents and pass them along to others. Be shrewd with your talents and you will be given even more!
Now, where is my knife sharpener?

Year A
Our Lord Jesus Christ, King of the Universe
November 22, 2020

Ezekiel 34:11-12, 15-17 / Psalm 23:1-2, 2-3, 5-6

Being Shepherded

Anyone who has taken a trip by bus can relate to what it is like to be shepherded. At every stop, the group leader or teacher stands up at the front and announces the rules for the stop. Where you can go, how much time you have, and even perhaps pair you up with another person as a "travel buddy" to make sure no one gets lost. After the stop is complete and everyone is back on the bus, the leader begins counting everyone to make sure the correct number of people are seated. (Although ask Kevin in Home Alone about how that doesn't always work)!

Being shepherded in this situation can seem restrictive. You may not be able to see everything that you wanted to see or have enough time to appreciate the sights around you. On the plus side, you don't have to worry about coming up with an itinerary, driving, parking, or getting lost. Each person will judge the value of being shepherded by the experience, either good or bad.

The reading today from Ezekiel and the responsorial psalm both describe what it is like to shepherded by God. He will guide his sheep, tend them, care for them, protect them, and give them peace if they will allow themselves to be led by him (like being a good tourist on a bus trip). But he will also call out those that say they want him as their shepherd but then go their own way (like someone who constantly goes wandering off causing the tour to be delayed.)

When we allow ourselves to be shepherded by God, we may not get everything that we want in life because we are called to live our lives justly and not just do what we want. For some, that is a bad experience because they do not get to do whatever they want. But there will be many that will live their lives in the freedom of knowing that no matter what, their shepherd will never lead them to harm. What kind of sheep do you want to be? I hope this article wasn't too baaaaad!
Deacon Mike

Year B
First Sunday of Advent
November 29, 2020

Isaiah 63:16b-17, 19b; 64:2-7

The Creativity of God

Most of you know that I like working with wood. Give me an afternoon in the workshop with a project and a stack of wood and I am one happy guy! One of the reasons that woodworking is a good fit for me is because it is mathematical and logical. In order for a project to be successful, all of the pieces need to cut and shaped precisely. To use a comparison, woodworking is a lot like baking. The ingredients in baking have to be fairly precise for the finished product to turn out correctly. Other mediums are more like cooking where being creative with the ingredients can turn a good dish into a spectacular dish. Starting with the basic recipe and then adding this and that is much like a sculptor starting with a lump of clay and shaping it into something amazing.

I am always a little envious of those that can start with an idea and then bring that idea to life by twisting, bending, and shaping until the end piece reflects the image they intended. Every time I have tried to draw, paint, or sculpt, I start with a perfect vision of what I want the end result to be, but I just lack the creative vision to make it happen. It's like I can only see the part that I am working on and I cannot see beyond to what is next and then I just get frustrated that it is not turning out the way I had envisioned.

The reason that I bring this up is because at the end of the reading from Isaiah today the author uses the analogy that the Lord is the potter, and we are the clay. In a way, this brings me great comfort because the creator of the universe does not lack any creative vision! We can look around and see that God's creative ability is far beyond anybody's imagination. The end result will be perfect. What brings me a little discomfort is that in order for clay to be formed into something beautiful it has to be smashed, punched, twisted, torn, and shaped. We will need to be shaped and molded and that that process can be painful at times. Nobody really wants to go through that process. What remains is the question… do we have the courage to yield ourselves to the will of the potter and be shaped into the perfect person that God envisions us to be?

Now where did I put my spokeshave?

Deacon Mike

Year B
Second Sunday in Advent
December 6, 2020

2 Peter 3:8-14

Where Does the Time Go?

Having lived my life around the Great Lakes and having grown up in the early seventies, it should come as no surprise that the ballad The Wreck of the Edmund Fitzgerald written by Gordon Lightfoot gets special attention every time it comes up on my music stream (that's the new radio for those still using a flip phone.) The song tells the story of the last great shipwreck on the Great Lakes that happened in 1975. The one line in the song that moves me is… "Does anyone know where the love of God goes when the waves turns the minutes to hours?" My imagination kicks in and I can envision the crew enduring the storm pounding their vessel with each wave bringing just a little more fear that they would not make it. I imagine that time seemed to last forever for those men.

At the beginning of the second reading today, the author talks about the difference between our time and God's time. Even greater than minutes and hours, they say that for God, a day is like a thousand years and a thousand years is like one day. When we think about the enormity of God, it becomes easier to see this point of view. But the reading goes on to point out that the reason that God's time and our time don't always mesh is because God wants to give us every chance to find our way to him.

It is easy to lose faith when we feel like God is not listening to our prayers. We have a need; we reach out to our Creator for help and what we receive is silence. We feel our prayers are not being answered. But the author of 2 Peter points out that God is far more interested in our salvation than in granting us everything we ask for. So, the next time you feel like God is not answering your prayer, instead of wondering why God is not responding, maybe try asking, "God what else are you trying to give me?" Even though a response may seem to take forever, just remember that is only an instant in God's time.

I wonder… does God have to deal with Daylight Savings Time too?

Deacon Mike

Year B
Third Sunday of Advent
December 13, 2020

John 1:6-8, 19-28

Searching

I saw a post on Facebook the other day that had me laughing out loud. It said, "Shout out to everyone who can still remember their childhood phone number but can't remember the password they created yesterday!" It is a little scary how much I can relate to that statement! (825-2748). I know that as I age, I find myself spending increasing amounts of time searching for things: passwords, keys, reading glasses, tools… the list seems to get longer by the day! But as I search, I also find things that I wasn't looking for that comes in handy soon after I find them. For instance, if I wasn't looking for my keys, I wouldn't have found the flash drive I needed the next day or some other item that I had forgotten about. There is value in the search even if I don't find what I was looking for.

In the gospel today, the Jews send representatives to inquire who exactly this John who is baptizing in the river Jordan. Their search kind of comes up empty. Elijah? Nope. The prophet? Nope. The Christ? Nope. Even though they don't get the answer they are looking for, they get a great treasure instead. "I am making a path for the Lord". If they are paying attention, John tells them that the savior they have been waiting for is coming soon. They found something that they were not looking for!

I think that almost everyone has gone through a time in their life when they were searching for the deeper things of life. Unfortunately, it seems that many who are searching are not open to finding what they may not be looking for and that keeps them from finding what God might be trying to give them. During these last days of Advent, maybe take the time to do some searching, but be ready to find something you were not looking for!

Hey look! That's where I put my library card!
Deacon Mike

Year B
Fourth Sunday of Advent
December 20, 2020

2 Samuel 7:1-5, 8B-12, 14A, 16

Home is Where the Heart is

Due to the current coronavirus, it looks like celebrating
Christmas this year may be different than in recent years.
Travels may be curtailed, gatherings may be smaller, some
family members may not be able to participate like they have in
the past, and venues may not be the same. However, if we are
focused on what this Christmas might be missing, we may lose
sight of what this Christmas is bringing. Namely, that the gift of
our Savior is going to be given to every man, woman, and child.

In the reading from 2 Samuel today, King David is living in a time
of relative peace and security. It comes to his mind that the ark
of the Covenant is dwelling in a tent (literally) while he is secure
in his home made of wood. He sets off to build a structure worthy
of God for the ark, but because he has shed much blood, God
tells Nathan the prophet that David's son Solomon will be the
one to build the temple. God also reminds Nathan of all the great
things he has done for the Israelites and that he does not need a
home of wood but needs to dwell in the hearts of everyone.

Whether you are with family this Christmas or not, whether you
are able to attend Mass at Christmas or not, whether it feels like
Christmas or not… try to remember that love always lives in the
heart and that is exactly where you can find Jesus. Our Savior
reigns!

Deacon Mike

Year B
Feast of the Holy Family of Jesus, Mary, and Joseph
December 27, 2020

Psalm 128:1-5.

Enjoy Your Handiwork!

I saw a picture frame recently that had me laughing out loud. The frame had one side shorter than what it should have been and the sign in the middle of the frame said, "Measure twice, cut once!" As a woodworker, I could totally relate! Sometimes you put your best effort into something, and it doesn't come out quite right. Then comes the choice… try again or do something different. Many times, the decision is based on the project and how prominent it is. If it is something that is for personal use and no one else will see it, the strategy might be to see what can be done to make it "usable." If the project will be seen by others, more drastic measures may be needed because it is a reflection on the maker's integrity and skill.

One of the lines in today's responsorial psalm says, "For you shall eat the fruit of your handiwork; blessed shall you be and favored."

This is a good reminder that as we maneuver through our life, it will only be as good as we build it. If we build our life with faith, hope, and love, we will enjoy our handiwork. If we build our life with fear, anxiety, and anger, we will have to live with that outcome too. To "measure twice, cut once" in life means to examine our choices carefully because what we really desire is a good outcome. But even if the outcome isn't what we desire, we have to decide if we are going to live with the flaw or do we go back an try again? Maybe a good question to ask is if the first choice was made out of faith, hope, and love or was it made out of fear, anxiety, and anger? Remember, you will eat the fruit of your handiwork.

May everyone have a blessed and wonderful new year!

Deacon Mike

Year B
Epiphany of the Lord
January 3, 2021

Matthew 2:1-12

Be a Star!

From the early days of television, talent shows have been around in one form or another. Some of the shows focus on a particular talent (like singing) while others are as varied as the talents the contestants bring to the stage. It can be amazing to see what people have trained themselves to accomplish. While the performances are varied, the one thing that all the contestants have in common is that they are looking for recognition and stardom. They want to be the talent that others aspire to be.

Today, we celebrate the Epiphany of the Lord. The story from Matthew is a familiar one with the magi coming from the east in search of a newborn king. Many assume that these men were familiar with astrology because they are guided by a star to the place where they find the child Jesus. In a time and place with few roads, miles of empty spaces, and no compass or GPS, the star is crucial for them to find what they are looking for.

There are many in our world today that lack the necessary tools to navigate through life. They may have not had any direction early on in life, they may have experienced some sort of physical or mental trauma, some sort of addiction, or maybe a combination of many things that have them in need of direction in their life. We may think that we lack the scientific training to the help them and so we leave it up to the "professionals" and in some cases that is what is needed. But in some cases, all they need is a star. Someone who shines brightly in their life to help guide them towards Jesus. Unlike those taking part in a talent show, you don't have to be the best... you just have to be the best version of yourself.

PS. I am looking for a volunteer... I recently lost my assistant in my knife throwing act.

Deacon Mike

Year B
Baptism of the Lord
January 10, 2021

Mark 1: 7-11

Using Your "Inside Voice"

I am sure that most of us have been in a store or restaurant when a child gets excited and their talking starts to get louder and louder until one of the parents tells them to use their "inside voice". (Who knows, maybe it has been used on you a time or two)! It is a reminder to be respectful of other people, but it has a secondary benefit too. When talking loudly, sometimes the message gets lost in the volume. People are so focused on how loudly someone is talking that they really are not paying attention to what is being said even if it is important. Sometimes how something is communicated is as important as what is being communicated.

I think that there are many people who like to talk "loudly" because they think it will help to draw attention to their message. In the short-term maybe it does, but over time I think that many begin to tune out because the volume of the message is just too loud. The message may be good, but it gets lost in the volume. In our dealings with others, it is important to be aware that how we come across can be just as important as what we have to say. If our message is good and right, and just, it should be able to stand on its own. That's why it is important that we take the time to work on our relationship with Jesus.

Today we celebrate the Baptism of the Lord. The Greek root of baptism is "baptismo" which means "immersed". If we keep ourselves in tune with scripture and the teachings of the Church, then we put ourselves in the best position to be immersed (baptized) in Christ and make our message to the world be right and just. Jesus enters the water to show us the way but it up to us to follow him. I think that Jesus often used his "inside voice" to show others the way. If we stay close to him, we too can use our inside voice to change our world.

Deacon Mike

Year B
Second Sunday in Ordinary Time
January 17, 2021

1 Samuel 3:3b-10, 19

So, You're a Wise Guy Eh?

Growing up, one of the rights of passage was to watch The Three Stooges. Larry, Mo, and Curly (I'm not a big Shemp fan) would have us youngsters in stitches. I have to admit there are several sketches that continue to take up space in my head (along with my childhood phone number). One of things I remember is when the Stooges would be in bed and Curly would start his goofy snoring and Mo would inevitably bonk Curly on the head and say, "wake up and go to sleep!" to get Curly to stop snoring. This came to mind as I read the first reading with Samuel waking up Eli twice only to be told to go back to bed.

While there is a common denominator in these two scenes of someone being awaken from their sleep, they differ in magnitude in the seriousness of the situation. One situation is so stupid it is funny and the other offers some food for thought.

The story of Samuel and Eli should bring us comfort and make us uneasy at the same time. We should find comfort in the fact that many people have a hard time recognizing when God is calling them. Samuel hears the voice of God and still cannot recognize he is being called. If you ever feel frustrated by trying to find out what God is telling you, remember this story! What should make us a little uneasy, however, is that God does not stop trying. Through our prayer life, our worship, and our family and friends, God is always calling us and waiting for that one response, "speak Lord, your servant is listening."

The next time you wake up in the middle of the night, maybe take some time to listen… someone may be calling your name!

Sleep tight!
Deacon Mike